CONSEQUENCES OF DISOBEDIENCE

A Journey Into The Heart Of Choices

TABLE OF CONTENTS

Introduction.. 1

Chapter 1: The Disobedience Towards God 4

Chapter 2: The Disobedience of the Law... 13

Chapter 3: The Disobedience of Principles....................................... 25

Chapter 4: The Disobedience of Marriage.. 35

Chapter 5: The Disobedience of Children... 42

Chapter 6: The Disobedience of Society... 46

Chapter 7: The Disobedience of Love 53

Chapter 8: The Disobedience of Leadership..................................... 59

Chapter 9: The Disobedience of Nations 64

Chapter 10: The Disobedience of Worship.. 69

Chapter 11: The Disobedience of Faith... 74

Chapter 12: The Disobedience of Truth.. 79

Chapter 13: The Disobedience of Integrity 84

Chapter 14: The Disobedience of Stewardship................................. 88

Chapter 15: The Path Back to Obedience 92

Conclusion.. 96

References... 97

INTRODUCTION

In a world where chaos, hatred, violence, anger, aggressive behavior, and many other negative actions, behaviors, and choices exist, many seek to understand why there exist destruction, poverty, diseases, corruption, deaths, and many other harmful effects humanity and other forms of life experience such tragic and heartfelt loss. Could it be the cause of disobedience? What other choices could have caused the inhabitants of Earth to embrace and endure and experience an abundance of disorder, lawlessness, and expiration?

Disobedience is one of the earliest and most enduring struggles of humanity. It is not just a matter of ignoring rules or commands; it reflects a human heart that resists authority, prioritizes self, and often rejects the wisdom of God. Disobedience has always carried weight, and its effects reach far beyond the individual who commits it. From the first act of defiance in the Garden of Eden to the moral struggles of modern nations, the thread of disobedience weaves itself into every era of human history. At its core, disobedience is more than breaking a rule—it is an act of rebellion against the order, wisdom, and love of God.

When we examine the root of disobedience, we find pride, selfishness, fear, and unbelief. These heart-postures lead us away from trust in God's Word and into paths that may seem appealing in the moment but result in consequences that often stretch across generations. The Bible makes this abundantly clear. Adam and Eve's disobedience introduced death, pain, and toil into the world. Saul lost his kingship because of his refusal to follow God's instructions completely. David's moment of weakness not only led to the death of Uriah but also to turmoil in his own family. Jonah's attempt to run from God nearly cost the lives of the sailors who unknowingly carried him. Each of these examples reveals a sobering truth: no act of disobedience is isolated, and no consequence is without ripple effects.

But the problem of disobedience is not confined to ancient texts. Our world today bears living testimony to its destructive power. We see it in broken marriages, rebellious children, corrupt governments, and collapsing societies. Every crime, every war, every act of injustice, every fractured family has its roots in some form of disobedience—whether to God, to moral principles, or to just laws. Humanity continues to repeat the cycle of disobedience, hoping somehow that the consequences will be different this time. Yet history, Scripture, and lived experience teach us that rebellion against divine order always ends in suffering.

This book seeks to explore the consequences of disobedience holistically. Each chapter unpacks a particular dimension of disobedience: toward God, toward His law, within marriage and family, in society at large, in leadership, in nations, and even in matters of faith, love, and truth. Together, these explorations create a picture of how disobedience erodes our lives from the inside out. The final chapter guides us toward "The Path Back to Obedience," showing that while disobedience carries weighty consequences, God's mercy and grace are always greater.

Yet the aim here is not despair but hope. For every act of disobedience, there is an opportunity for repentance. For every broken covenant, there is a pathway back to restoration. Our rebellion does not diminish God's grace; instead, His mercy shines brighter against the backdrop of human failure. The final chapter, "The Path Back to Obedience," provides practical guidance for returning to alignment with God's will—through humility, repentance, faith, and daily surrender.

Obedience is not meant to restrict us but to protect and bless us. God's laws and principles are not cages, but compasses—guiding us toward life, joy, peace, and fulfillment. To obey is to choose life. To disobey is to invite destruction. The stakes could not be higher, for our choices not only shape our own destinies but also the futures of our families, communities, and nations.

As you embark on this journey through the following chapters, may you be reminded of the seriousness of disobedience but also encouraged by the promise of redemption. For while disobedience brings consequences, obedience brings blessings. And where sin abounds, grace abounds even more.

CHAPTER 1:

THE DISOBEDIENCE TOWARDS GOD

Disobedience towards God is the foundation of all other forms of disobedience. The very first act of rebellion in human history occurred in the Garden of Eden when Adam and Eve disobeyed God's direct command not to eat from the tree of the knowledge of good and evil. Their choice not only altered their own lives but set into motion consequences that continue to shape humanity today.

God created Adam and Eve with free will. He did not design them as robots who could only obey; He gave them the ability to choose. That choice came with responsibility. In Genesis 2:16-17, God commanded Adam, "You are free to eat from any tree in the garden; but you must not eat from the tree of the knowledge of good and evil, for when you eat from it you will certainly die." This command was simple, clear, and reasonable. Yet, when the serpent tempted Eve, she chose to question God's word, and Adam followed her in disobedience.

The result was devastating. Their eyes were opened, but not in the way they had hoped. They became aware of their nakedness, ashamed of their condition, and separated from the presence of God. They were expelled from the Garden of Eden, and death entered the human story. Romans 5:12 explains, "Sin entered the world through one man, and death through sin, and in this way, death came to all people, because all sinned." The consequence of one act of disobedience has reverberated through every generation since.

Many of our choices in life are influenced by people who think they have the right intentions, places that seem to foster our sense of belonging, and things that may satisfy our needs. However, any of our choices that guide us to disobey God will always result in a negative consequence. Furthermore, we must believe that God is in control of everything and that what He has commanded is for His purpose and our good, regardless of the outlook on things, the movement of time, and the downfall of humanity. Remember, it is our choices that result in our consequences.

Before their choice to disobey, they communed with God in the midst of the garden, having free rein to every tree in the garden except the one tree God gave command not to touch. It has been asked that "If God knew man was going to fail, why did He place that tree in the garden?" First and foremost, God did not create robots as humans. He blessed us in His likeness to possess intellect, discernment, creativity, beauty, and power to make good choices in respectful obedience to Him. Adam didn't fail; he just failed to obey and follow instructions.

Disobedience towards God continues to take many forms today. It may be subtle, such as ignoring His voice when He calls us to act in faith, or it may be blatant, such as rejecting His Word altogether. Moses provides another example. In Numbers 20, God instructed Moses to speak to the rock to bring forth water for the Israelites. Instead, Moses struck the rock twice in anger. Though water flowed, his disobedience cost him the privilege of entering the Promised Land. This shows that even partial or altered obedience is still disobedience in God's eyes.

There is a very significant lesson in this story of Moses. We learn that God is very specific in giving commands. Therefore, we should never think that what He said about one thing also applies to the next. Always check with God on His directions, details and instructions. Furthermore, uncontrolled anger can lead to disobedience and often cause harm or disasters. God said that Moses's disobedience broke his faith with God and did not treat God as holy. Unfortunately, we do not know what our disobedience to God looks like or how He perceives it. Consequently, the promises of God are possessed through obedience.

King Saul also illustrates this truth of disobedience. In 1 Samuel 13 and 15, Saul disobeyed God's instructions by offering sacrifices himself instead of waiting for Samuel and by sparing King Agag and the best of the Amalekites' livestock, though God commanded their destruction. His actions led to the loss of his kingdom and the removal of God's Spirit from his life. Saul's disobedience reveals how pride, fear of people, and impatience often lead us to dishonor God.

Impatience is another negative trait that can lead one into disobedience. Wherefore, we must know when to wait on God or when He is waiting on us. Secondly, never let anyone move you to make a choice by force, coercion, or manipulation. Fear is another factor that leads to misleading choices and disobedience. "Saul's disobedience serves as a cautionary tale about the consequences of failing to trust and obey God fully. His actions reveal a heart that is more concerned with outward appearances and human approval than with genuine submission to divine authority (Bible Hub 2004-2025)."

And Samuel said, Hath the LORD as great delight in burnt offerings and sacrifices, as in obeying the voice of the LORD? Behold, to obey is better than sacrifice, and to hearken than the fat of rams. For rebellion is as the sin of witchcraft, and stubbornness is as iniquity and idolatry. Because thou hast rejected the word of the LORD, he hath also rejected thee from being king. And Saul said unto Samuel, I have sinned: for I have transgressed the commandment of the LORD, and thy words: because I feared the people, and obeyed their voice (1 Sam 15:22-24 KVJ).

Samuel proclaimed to Saul that it is better to obey than to sacrifice, and to listen is better than offering the best part of the sacrifice. Note how God viewed his disobedience as rebellion and stubbornness. When God states to remove, get rid of, or crucify, we must hearken to His command because it can be viewed as rebellion. And rebellion may result in God removing you from a position, placing an ungodly ruler over a nation or rejecting our prayers and supplications. Although Saul was king for 40 years, God removed His Spirit from him after 2 years (1 Samuel 13:1). You might think God doesn't notice our disobedience because we are doing fine and going about life; nevertheless, we ought to examine ourselves, take heed of any disobedience, and repent.

David, though called "a man after God's own heart," also disobeyed when he committed adultery with Bathsheba and arranged the death of her husband, Uriah (2 Samuel 11). His disobedience led to death, family turmoil, and national consequences. That disobedience also led to him losing a child. As harmful as that may come across to some people, it will never compare to all of the murders we have committed against children. David shows us how human nature (carnal man) is set to disobey God, no matter the relationship we have with God.

Nevertheless, David was the most repenting, seeking forgiveness, and pouring all of his heart and failures out to God. Disobedience may have consequences, but a heart set forth to confession and repentance can bring restoration, deliverance, and peace with God. Even so, if we take heed of the lessons and examples that came before us, we should make better decisions.

. "And David said unto God, Is it not I that commanded the people to be numbered? Even I it is who have sinned and done evil indeed; but as for these sheep, what have they done? Let thine hand, I pray thee, O LORD my God, be on me, and on my father's house; but not on thy people, that they should be plagued (1 Chron 21:17). David's disobedience resulted in the suffering of many innocent people. And we question why bad things happen to good people. Do not be deceived into believing your choices will only affect you.

"David's disobedience serves as a reminder of the complexities of human nature and the importance of accountability. His story illustrates that leaders must be vigilant in their decisions, as their actions can have far-reaching consequences. Additionally, David's eventual repentance and return to God highlight the possibility of redemption and the importance of seeking forgiveness after wrongdoing (Bible Hub 2025)." "Those who accept positions of leadership cannot evade responsibility for the effects of their actions on others (Baker, Houseman, Matthews, 2014)." The consequences of David's disobedience resulted in God given him three choices: (1) three years of famine, or (2) three months of devastation by the sword of his enemies, or (3) three days of a pestilence on the land. David chose the third option, and 70,000 people died.

Jonah disobeyed God's call to preach to Nineveh and fled in the opposite direction. His disobedience endangered those around him until God intervened with a storm and a great fish. When we deliberately choose to disobey God, as Jonah did, the consequences may result in pain, suffering, or the loss of something. If God calls you to do something or just wants your attention, it is best that you take heed and say as Samuel said, "Speak Lord, for thy servant is listening." Consequently, if God has to come chasing after you, trust, you are not going to like whatever He decides to do.

God called me to ministry twice, and I tried to run like Jonah and put myself in the hospital numerous times. When I share my testimony with some Christians, they often say they don't believe God would do any harm to me. Nevertheless, I know it was God, and His grace sustained, healed, and gave me the power to write this book. Back to the story of Jonah, the text said he tried to flee from the presence of the Lord. Let me save you some time and energy. No one can flee from the Omnipresent God. The Psalmist states, "Whither shall I go from thy spirit? Or whither shall I flee from thy presence? If I ascend up into heaven, thou art there: if I make my bed in hell, behold, thou art there (Psalm 139:7-8). So Jonah's disobedience caused God to swallow him up in a whale's belly for three days and three nights. He cried out regarding his affliction unto God, and he says his soul fainted. Oh, how we are quick to call on God in our afflictions, distress, and anguish when all we must do is obey. God was not finished with him yet.

In chapter three, God gives Jonah the command a second time to go preach to the city of Nineveh and this time he obeyed. I wished I had obeyed the second time. Another failure in disobeying God's command to go speak to someone or some people is the loss of souls being won to Christ. It's not even about knowing the right words to say; it's about being obedient to God and allowing the Holy Spirit to speak through you. Furthermore, Jonah tells God that he ran because he knew God was a merciful, gracious God of great kindness and embraces repentance (Chapter 4). The Bible says Jonah was very angry towards God for saving the city of Nineveh. As stated before, never let your anger make you disobedient. Always remember, we cannot determine the consequences.

These stories remind us that disobedience towards God is not just about breaking rules; it is about breaking a relationship. To disobey God is to reject His authority, His wisdom, and His love. It demonstrates a lack of trust in His character and plan. The consequences are separation, loss of blessing, and often harm to ourselves and others.

There are many other stories of disobedience towards God. I could write a book just on the disobedience of the children of Israel. Moreover, many kings such as Solomon, Jeroboam and Ahab disobeyed God and caused harm to innocent people and corrupted nations. In the New Testament, we read of the Pharisee, Ananias and Sapphira, and even the Apostle Paul (Saul) displayed disobedience towards God. Even today, the disobedience of many, including those who claim Christ as their Lord and Savior, is worse than in the days of the Old Testament. I have watched a lot of YouTube videos and other podcasts about what it would take to make the world better, or even for the church to function as Christians. First, it starts with obeying the Word of God. Secondly, we, as Christians, are not seeking to be better; we are seeking righteousness. Thirdly, learn to listen to the Bible and not just read it. The bible clearly states, "So then faith cometh by hearing, and hearing by the word of God (Romans 10:17)."

Yet, even in the midst of disobedience, God's grace remains. God clothed Adam and Eve before leaving Eden. David found forgiveness after repentance. Jonah was given a second chance to obey. These examples highlight that while disobedience carries consequences, repentance restores us to fellowship with God.

The lesson is clear: disobedience towards God leads to separation, suffering, and loss, but obedience leads to blessing, purpose, and life. To obey God is to walk in alignment with His will, which is always for our good.

CHAPTER 2:

THE DISOBEDIENCE OF THE LAW

The law of God is His revealed standard of righteousness. It was given to guide, protect, and bless His people. The Ten Commandments, written by the very finger of God, stand as eternal principles of moral order. To disobey these laws is not only to disregard rules but to reject the wisdom and holiness of God.

"To disobey God is not merely to break a rule—it is to reject wisdom, love, and life itself. Divine law is not a cage; it is a compass. And when we ignore it, we drift into chaos." The Hebrew word for law is "Tora," meaning "instructions and the Greek word is (nomos), meaning direction and instructions. Furthermore, the word law appears in the Bible over 400 times. Accordingly, the laws written in the Bible are for direction and instruction on God's will, His commandments, and His design for creation. Without laws such as the Constitution or the Bible, what would we have to govern our way of life? A general example is the speed limit posted on roadways. If no speed limit is set to govern the flow of traffic while protecting pedestrians, a massive number of vehicular fatalities and casualties will result in uncontrolled deaths, emotional trauma, and grief faced by survivors and families. Therefore, disobedience of the law is set to produce the same ramifications.

Walter Elwell wrote in the Baker's Evangelical Dictionary of Biblical Theology, "the role of law is to administrate the covenant. Laws prohibit things destructive to a relationship with God (e.g., worshiping other gods). The law provides direction on what a loving response to God should be and explains how to reap the full benefits of the relationship. From one perspective, the promises formalized by the covenant were unconditional; from an individual's perspective, benefits could be forfeited by disobedience. Disobedience does not automatically invalidate a covenant, any more than a husband's rudeness to a wife he vowed to cherish invalidates his marriage covenant. Yet disobedience mars the relationship and may reduce its benefits. In the desert, a whole generation of Israelites forfeited their covenant benefits (the promised land) through disobedience, yet the covenant continued (El-well 1996)."

The law serves as a mirror, showing us God's character and our own sinfulness. Romans 7:7 declares, "I would not have known what sin was had it not been for the law." The law was never meant to be a burden but a guide to lead us toward life and holiness. Yet, humanity has repeatedly disobeyed God's laws, with disastrous results.

Disobedience has broken the covenant and brought about the destructive things the law was meant to prohibit. Jesus Christ is the only Mediator and Redeemer of the relationship with God. Even so, He says, "And why call ye me, Lord, Lord, and do not the things which I say?" (Luke 6:46) Walter also says God's promises were unconditional, and the benefits of inheriting them were forfeited because of disobedience. Stop for a minute and think about the promises of God and compare them to the world we live in now. This is the very reason many claim God does not exist, or if there is a God, then why are people and things so destructive, hatred, self-righteousness, death, diseases, poverty, and many other evils exist. The answer is disobedience. Deuteronomy 12:8 explains it well: "You shall not do according to all that we are doing here today, everyone doing whatever is right in his own eyes. I will elaborate later in this chapter regarding the disobedience of commandments that forfeit promises. First, let us journey to the most imperative command given by God, the Sabbath.

The Sabbath command, for example, was instituted not as a restriction but as a gift. God Himself rested on the seventh day and blessed it as holy. Yet, Israel often disregarded the Sabbath, choosing work, commerce, and pleasure over honoring God's Day. Their disobedience brought judgment upon the nation.

The Sabbath is far greater than a covenant. The Sabbath was instituted before the Ten Commandments were written, and it was established before sin entered the world. The Sabbath is part of creation; therefore, the Sabbath should be part of us all. We were created in the six-day work week of God, and Genesis 2 completes the creation week with "Thus the heavens and the earth were finished, and all the host of them. And on the seventh day God ended his work which he had made; and he rested on the seventh day from all his work which he had made. And God blessed the seventh day and sanctified it: because that in it he had rested from all his work which God created and made." Being mentioned only about 130 times in the Bible, do yourself a favor and read about the consequences of disobeying the Sabbath, and compare them to the decline of the world's civilization.

This divine ordinance carries significant consequences for violating the covenant relationship with God. The disobedience of the Sabbath has contributed to many avoidable negative outcomes. Words cannot express how sacred, crucial and vital it is to keep the Sabbath and observe it in holiness and sanctification. While many have no idea of its sacredness, others believe that the Sabbath was done away with Jesus' death on the cross, and some even think that Sunday is their Sabbath. There is nowhere in the Bible that states the Sabbath was moved to Sunday or that it is no longer necessary to honor and keep the Sab-bath. Saturday worship was changed to Sunday by the Roman Emperor Constantine in A.D. 321. And because Western Civilization (America) adopted Roman Catholic principles and doctrines, Sunday worshippers are conditioned to worship on Sunday. This covenant violation has led to divine judgment, and there would be fewer deaths if we honored His covenant day of rest.

Here are some scripture to enlighten the importance of Sabbath keeping; Exodus 20:8-11, 31:12-17, 35:2, Leviticus 23:3, 24:8, 25:2, Numbers 15:32, Deuteronomy 5:12, 14-15, Nehemiah 9:14, 13:15-22,

Isaiah 56:2,6, 58:13, 66:23, Jeremiah 17:21-22, 24, 27, Ezekiel 20:12-13, 16, 20-21, 24, 22:8, 26, 23:38, 44:24, Mat-thew 12:1, 8, Mark 2:27-28, Acts 16:13. All contain the sacred importance in keeping the Sabbath and the consequences following disobedience. Moreover, Jesus, His disciples, the Apostle Paul, and everyone who honors God kept the Sabbath. The Sabbath is the fourth commandment in the Ten Commandments as a law and covenant. Exodus 31 conveys the Sabbath law, and Nehemiah and Jesus became angry over the profaning of the Sabbath. Many talk about and hope for a better world, may we start with the Sabbath and keep it holy.

Next, let us journey through the Ten Commandments and discover the heart of God in governing what is best for His children. The Ten Commandments appear first in Exodus 20:3-17 and were written with the finger of God (Exodus 31:18), not by Moses or man. There is a debate about the Ten Commandments being done away with Christ's death and Apostle Paul mentioning that the saints (children of God) are no longer under the law but under grace. We shall explore the universal command to keep the law (Ten Commandments) forever. "The Ten Commandments are foundational to God's moral law. Breaking them isn't just disobedience—it's a spiritual danger (Wilson, 2025)." Disobeying the Ten Commandments can lead to a range of consequences, both immediate and long-term.

The First Commandment declares, "You shall have no other gods before me." Disobedience to this law led Israel into idolatry, worshipping Baal, golden calves, and other false gods. The result was divine judgment, foreign captivity, and national ruin. The choice to disobey this commandment means we're setting something or someone else above God in our lives. There are many religions in the world; however, there's only one true God — the Father, the Creator, Who is a jealous God. It's very sad and tragic how many people in the world say there is no God or that God doesn't exist. Disobedience and Satan have been the culprits in causing many Christians to stumble, disobey, and behave like they never read the Bible or listen to a sermon on obeying the Word of God. Others have become disobedient and rebellious because a prayer wasn't answered or because God didn't fulfill their request.

According to Jesus, "thou shalt love the Lord thy God with all thy heart, and with all thy soul, and with all thy mind." (Matthew 22:37) Do we believe that God is deserving of our all? To put God at the forefront of every decision, every choice and every action tells God, "For the joy of the Lord is my strength." (Nehemiah 8:10) Otherwise, disobedience is present to steal your joy and lead you to negative consequences. In Exodus 23, God gives instructions to the Israelites on what is righteous and moral in His lordship. God declares that the obedience in doing all that He has spoken will result in sovereign protection, divine provision, and long life. Furthermore, in disobedience, God's protection may be removed, there may be a shortage of provision, and a short-lived, frustrated life may result.

The Second Commandment has a strong consequence for making any graven image and bowing down or worshipping any type of idol. He states, "visiting the iniquity of the fathers upon the children unto the third and fourth generation of them that hate me; And shewing mercy unto thousands of them that love me and keep my commandments. (Exodus 20:5-6)." It's obvious that if you hate God, you are destined to disobey Him, and I pray that we are very conscious and take heed that He said He would punish our children to the third and fourth generation.. The Third Commandment declares, "Thou shalt not take the name of the LORD thy God in vain." This commandment is all about respect and reverence for God. In a world where disrespect is becoming common, it's no wonder that we use the name of God in any manner that fits our pleasure. The rest of the commandment says He will not hold you guiltless. Therefore, taking the name of God in vain is guilty of causing anxiety, stress, sadness, sorrow, low self-esteem, etc.

The Fourth Commandment, remembering the Sabbath, as mentioned earlier in the chapter, is imperative to keep. Although if we transgress one commandment, we are said to be breaking all of them. One other point I would like to make regarding the fourth commandment is the word "remember." If we are told to remember the Sabbath day, evidently the Sabbath was already instituted and should be set apart as a holy day of rest. "Honor your father and your mother, so that you may live long in the land the Lord your God is giving you." This is the Fifth Commandment that should be embedded in our hearts, whether we believe that sometimes parents do not deserve respect and honor. The consequences of dishonor in the world today have, unfortunately, shortened life. As Ecclesiastes 7:17 proclaims, "Why shouldest thou die before thy time?"

The Sixth Commandment declares, "Thou shalt not kill." Murder and hatred, and violence are so rampant that the consequences are self-explanatory, while death is ripping through humanity at a rapid rate. Disobeying the command against murder filled the land with violence. The only cure is obedience and the love of God in Jesus Christ. Next is the Seventh Commandment, which states "thou shalt not commit adultery." We will explore the marriage journey in chapter four.

Nevertheless, God instituted marriage for the sacredness of love, unity, purpose, and faith. Adultery is a sin that has caused much harm to the body, emotions, spirit, and soul. Consequently, the struggle with sexual functions, diseases, viruses, and cardiovascular problems is the outcome of disobedience. Commandment Eight: "Thou shalt not steal." Do we realize that when we steal, we are literally saying what's yours is mine without remorse, no reasoning, or no compassion for the individual, community, or God?

The Ninth Commandment is "thou shalt not bear false witness against thy neighbor." Listen, in Revelation 21, it is written that liars will not inherit the Kingdom of God, nor enter eternal life, nor have their names written in the Lamb's book of life. Therefore, bearing false witness may result in severe damage to relationships, erosion of trust, mistrust, division, and conflict among individuals and groups, or harm to innocent individuals and undermine justice and fairness. The Tenth and final Commandment expresses "Thou shalt not covet thy neighbour's house, thou shalt not covet thy neighbour's wife, nor his manservant, nor his maidservant, nor his ox, nor his ass, nor any thing that is thy neighbor's." God created each individual in His own unique likeness, and He has given us everything that pertains to life and godliness. Additionally, there are enough resources, food, materials, and water to sustain our world.

Unfortunately, "for all that is in the world, the lust of the flesh, and the lust of the eyes, and the pride of life," (1 Jn 2:16) causes us to focus on what we lack and miss appreciating what we already have. In which, never being satisfied can lead to perpetual discontent and a lack of enjoyment in life. The consequences that follow are poor financial decisions, theft, adultery, and the removal of God's blessings and His Holy Spirit. "God has given us His holy precepts, because He loves mankind. To shield us from the results of transgression. He reveals the principles of righteousness. Since "the law of the Lord is perfect," every variation from it must be evil. Those who disobey the commandments of God and teach others to do so are condemned by Christ. The Savior's life of obedience maintained the claims of the law;

it proved that the law could be kept in humanity and showed the excellence of character that obedience would develop." DA 308, 309

In the New Testament, Jesus reaffirmed the importance of God's law. He declared in Matthew 5:17, "Do not think that I have come to abolish the Law or the Prophets; I have not come to abolish them but to fulfill them. "For many believe that He fulfilled the law when He died and was resurrected, and therefore we are not under the law but grace (Romans 6:14). If we are no longer need the law of God, by what standard are we living? What principles are in place to govern societies? Without the law, what would be the need for grace? Sin identifies the breaking of the law. There are too many occurrences of keeping the commandments throughout the Bible. Furthermore, the same writer of Romans 6:14 also wrote, "What shall we say then? Is the law sin? God forbid. Nay, I had not known sin, but by the law: for I had not known lust, except the law had said, Thou shalt not covet Romans 7:7. Wherefore the law is holy, and the commandment holy, and just, and good (verse 12)." What law and commandment is the Apostle Paul referring to? Lastly, in 1 Corinthians 7:19, it is written, Circumcision is nothing, and uncircumcision is nothing, but the keeping of the commandments of God.

The Ten Commandments form the foundation of God's law (Exodus 20:1–17). Israel repeatedly disobeyed these commands, turning to idols (Exodus 32), profaning the Sabbath (Jeremiah 17:21–23), and dishonoring their parents. The results were captivity and national ruin. Modern parallels can be seen in widespread dishonesty, broken homes, and lawlessness. Just as ignoring traffic laws causes accidents, ignoring God's laws brings destruction.

The consequences of disobeying God's law are not only spiritual but also practical. A society that disregards God's moral order experiences corruption, crime, poverty, and despair. Without a foundation of truth, every person does what is right in their own eyes, leading to chaos. Obedience to the law, however, must flow from love. Jesus summarized the entire law in two commands: "Love the Lord your God with all your heart, soul, and mind, and love your neighbor as yourself" (Matthew 22:37–39).

Disobedience of the law, therefore, is ultimately disobedience of love. When we lie, steal, covet, or dishonor others, we show a lack of love for God and people. The consequence is broken relationships, mistrust, and separation from God's presence.

The consequences of disobedience to law shall bring severe judgment on humanity, an increase in diseases and poverty, and other personal and worldwide destruction. The Bible conveys that there is a way of curing disobedience. First, we must obey and follow this command; "If my people, which are called by my name, shall humble themselves, and pray, and seek my face, and turn from their wicked ways; then will I hear from heaven, and will forgive their sin, and will heal their land (2 Ch 7:14)." Next, in Deuteronomy 11:13-27, God declares blessings of rain and harvest, long life, protection from the enemy, and God's presence and Holy Spirit. Nevertheless, He also proclaimed a curse on all who disobey the commandments He set before us. "Let us hear the conclusion of the whole matter: Fear God and keep his commandments: for this is the whole duty of man. For God shall bring every work into judgment, with every secret thing, whether it be good, or whether it be evil (Ecclesiastes 12:13-14).

Yet, through Christ, we are empowered to obey. The Holy Spirit writes God's law on our hearts and enables us to live in righteousness. Obedience to the law is no longer about external conformity but about internal transformation.

The lesson is clear: disobedience of the law brings disorder, destruction, and death, but obedience brings blessing, order, and life.

CHAPTER 3:

THE DISOBEDIENCE OF PRINCIPLES

A principle is defined as a comprehensive and fundamental law, doctrine, or assumption that governs behavior or actions, a basic idea or rule that explains or controls how something happens or works, a moral rule or belief that helps distinguish right from wrong, influencing actions, or an essential quality or doctrine that serves as a foundation for a system of beliefs or behaviors. Principles are foundational truths that guide behavior and decisions. In Scripture, principles include holiness, righteousness, faith, integrity, and wisdom. To disregard these principles is to invite confusion and destruction into life.

Disobeying the principles of ethics, morals, rules, and God's Word can lead to serious consequences, including real-world suffering, inequality, exploitation, loss of miracles and blessings, and spiritual blindness and distancing from God. Proverbs is filled with divine principles that lead to blessing when obeyed and destruction when ignored. "The fear of the Lord is the beginning of wisdom" (Proverbs 1:7). When this principle is neglected, people act foolishly, lacking direction and discernment.

The book of Proverbs expresses many principles that lead to a fruitful life, while disobeying them will always lead to divine judgment and the destruction of the mind, body, and spirit. Furthermore, Proverbs explains the differences between the wise and foolish. Solomon, the author writing to his son Rehoboam (God writing to His children) began his discourse with "to know wisdom and instruction; to perceive the words of understanding; To receive the instruction of wisdom, justice, and judgment, and equity; To give subtilty to the simple, to the young man knowledge and discretion. A wise man will hear, and will increase learning; and a man of understanding shall attain unto wise counsels: To understand a proverb, and the interpretation; the words of the wise, and their dark sayings. The fear of the LORD is the beginning of knowledge: but fools despise wisdom and instruction (Proverbs 1:2-7).

Proverbs is filled with divine principles that lead to blessing when obeyed and destruction when ignored. When this principle is neglected, people act foolishly, lacking direction and discernment. It is imperative to understand that one must seek wisdom to apply it to whatever instructions are set before him or her. Thus, it is needed in righteously obeying principles.

Principles are moral rules or beliefs that help distinguish right from wrong and influence actions. In chapter five of Proverbs, it talks about the wrong choice of a strange woman (immoral, deceptive) as opposed to a wife (virtuous woman). Choosing to disobey the instructions to stay away from the strange woman may result in the ravishing of the strange woman, being consumed by wickedness and death hereinafter. The term "strange woman" can also refer to a harlot (prostitute). Unfortunately, the principles of marriage, no sex before marriage (fornication), and no sex outside of marriage (adultery) have become more disregarded as time proceeds. This disobedience to these principles has led to fornication, adultery, pornography, sexual immorality, and homosexuality. The consequences are as follows: diseases, emotional stress, destruction of the home life (family), and loss of life.

The principle of holiness is another example. God commands, "Be holy, because I am holy" (1 Peter 1:16). Holiness means being set apart for God, avoiding sin, and pursuing righteousness. Yet, when people disobey this principle, they embrace worldliness, immorality, and compromise. The result is loss of God's presence and power. The dismissal of holiness may sometimes hinder prayers from being answered, bring calamity to family, friends, and loved ones, cause mental and physical health issues, and lead to financial stress. Furthermore, we jeopardize embracing "the peace that surpasses all understanding" and place us in a state of loneliness, unhappiness, and His blessedness.

If we want to get to heaven—and we all do—then we must do all in our power to arrive at the holiness of life that God has called us to (Broom 2025).

"And ye shall be holy unto me: for I the LORD am holy, and have severed you from other people, that ye should be mine." (Leviticus 20:26) Holiness keeps us in the presence of God, and this principle has become lost to disobedience and resulted in God taking His favor off the people of God. Holiness is the nucleus of our faith and obedience to our Great God. We are daily striving and seeking, and pursuing to be like Jesus by being filled with holiness. Many are denying the sacredness of being holy and choosing the world, Satan, and other unholy principles to guide their life and behaviors at the stage of writing this book, wars, rumors of wars, teenage murders, mass shootings and stabbing, and other natural disasters plaguing humanity because of disobedience and not determining to be holy.

Sanctification is the principle that ushers us into holiness. Sanctification is the process of being sanctified (set apart) to be made holy. God told Moses in Exodus 31:13-14 to speak to the children of Israel about Him sanctifying them and to keep the Sabbath holy. They were sanctified as the Sabbath is sanctified, set apart from Sunday, which made Saturday a holy day, and they would be a holy people. In addition, Jesus prayed, "They are not of the world, even as I am not of the world. Sanctify them through thy truth: thy word is truth. As thou hast sent me into the world, even so have I also sent them into the world. And for their sakes I sanctify myself that they also might be sanctified through the truth. Neither pray I for these alone, but for them also which shall believe on me through their word (John 17:16-

20). The Word of God is truth, and the world is a lie. Therefore, if we are disobedient to sanctification, our lives will obviously be lived as a lie. The consequence is spiritual blindness, moral compromise, and distance from God.

There are numerous consequences for disobeying sanctification, such as, accessory to crime, evil (bad) choices, physical and mental abuse, negative influences, and being apart from God and all His promises. "Do not be deceived: "Evil company corrupts good habits (1 Corinthians 15:33 NKJV)." This passage of scripture warns against the influence of negative association on one's morals and behavior. It emphasizes that associating with individuals who engage in unethical or immoral behavior can erode one's character and values (Bible Hub).

"For this is the will of God, even your sanctification, that ye should abstain from fornica-tion: That every one of you should know how to possess his vessel in sanctification and honour (1 Thessalonians 4:3-4);" Listen, God does not have a will for each person (you have to know God's will for your life, preachers words). His will for all mankind is to be sanctified to Himself for holiness and righteousness. Although Apostle Paul pointed out one thing to be sanctified from, but "the works of the flesh are manifest, which are these; Adultery, fornication, uncleanness, lasciviousness, Idolatry, witchcraft, hatred, variance, emulations, wrath, strife, seditions, heresies, envying, murders, drunkenness, reveling, and such like: of the which I tell you before, as I have also told you in time past, that they which do such things shall not inherit the kingdom of God (Gal 5:19-21). All these corrupt sanctifications result in devastating consequences.

"Now the just shall live by faith: but if any man draw back, my soul shall have no pleasure in him (Hebrews 10:38)." The principle of justification has not taken root in the hearts of the people who claim Jesus Christ as their Lord and Savior. All who believe in their heart that God raised Him from the dead and confess with the mouth, you are saved and justified through His life. If we are called the "just", then why do we live as if we are condemned and not validated by the blood of Christ? Consequently, if we disobey living in justification, then we should live as though Jesus never came. In denying the principle of justification, it is like a man released from prison, but each day he awakens, he spends it on the prison grounds. As the verse stated, Jesus will have no pleasure in us, and the One Who made us free will see no fruit in the withered branch. Many Christians sing and shout that they have the victory; nevertheless, they live defeated lives.

(For many walk, of whom I have told you often, and now tell you even weeping, that they are the enemies of the cross of Christ: Whose end is destruction, whose God is their belly, and whose glory is in their shame, who mind earthly things (Philippians 3:18-19.) The consequences of failing to justify can cut deep into the soul and rob you of liberty, justice, and peace. "But if a man be just, and do that which is lawful and right, Hath walked in my statutes, and hath kept my judgments, to deal truly; he is just, he shall surely live, saith the

Lord GOD (Ezekiel 18:5, 9)." Unfortunately, we live in an unjust world, where Satan and injustice flaw the justice system. This is an urgent warning to the reader: seek Jesus and embrace the principle of justification to be made perfect and to reach towards the full stature of Christ. "Therefore, as by the offence of one judgment came upon all men to condemnation; even so by the righteousness of one the free gift came upon all men unto justification of life (Romans 5:18)."

"But seek ye first the kingdom of God, and his righteousness; and all these things shall be added unto you." (Matthew 6:33). Righteousness is of God and not of ourselves. Often, the response to one's failure or an evil choice is "I would like to do better." Now, I truly understand those words can be used for confidence; however, if we are to "be not conformed to this world: but be ye transformed by the renewing of your mind (Romans 12:1), it would be more beneficial to say "I want to be right (righteous) and not just better? Righteousness to the individual seems out of reach and unattainable. This world of sin has been captivated by so much disobedience that righteousness is nonexistent and dwells in the rearview mirror. Akin to justification, righteousness is also a principle that has not taken root in the heart of the believer. Many scholars and leaders will say, "We will never be righteous on this side of heaven or until we get to heaven. Why would Jesus tell us to seek His righteousness if it were not possible? Many of the things God conveys to us are not followed because of disbelief and self-righteousness.

"For as by one man's disobedience many were made sinners, so by the obedience of one shall many be made righteous." (Romans 5:19). If Christ made us righteous and our heart deceives us to disobey the righteous gift of living in the grace of God, subsequently, the consequences are communicated in Romans 1:18-32. Take heed to go and read those verses and see the disobedience and the consequences being manifested in our world today. Godliness and righteousness are very important principles we are to live by. As mentioned earlier, the only reason righteousness is not obtained is because of self-righteousness and not embracing the righteousness of Jesus Christ and Him only through the Holy Spirit. If you do not know how to seek His righteousness, ask by faith with a pure heart's desire.

"Behold, God is my salvation; I will trust, and not be afraid: for the LORD JEHOVAH is my strength and my song; he also is become my salvation." (Isaiah 12:2). Salvation is the principle that holds life together and carries the ministry forward in the spirit of the believer. On the condition that we choose to disobey our salvation, we are destined to live in laziness, immaturity, and a lack of the discernment and wisdom needed to overcome obstacles and to reach a place where nothing matters but Christ Jesus. "For he saith, I have heard thee in a time accepted, and in the day of salvation have I succored thee: behold, now is the ac-cepted time; behold, now is the day of salvation." (2 Cor 6:2) Every day we awaken is an ac-ceptable day of salvation and a purpose to "press toward the mark for the prize of the high calling of

God in Christ Jesus." (Phil 3:14) The introducing verse to this paragraph says that God and Jesus are our salvation and apart from Him we can do nothing.

"For God hath not appointed us to wrath, but to obtain salvation by our Lord Jesus Christ." (1 Thess 5:9). Some believe that our salvation is secure (once saved, forever saved). This false teaching and false belief are not the truth and will lead you into disobedience of your salvation. The belief indicated is erroneous and delusional, manipulating the individual into thinking they can do whatever they want or desire, with no consequences. They can ask God for forgiveness and go do it again and again. Nevertheless, that is when we will be appointed to His wrath, and we witness every day the tragedy and destruction of God's wrath and the consequences that follow.

Notably, we cannot choose or know which consequences will emerge, but calamity, catastrophe, adversity, afflictions, misfortune, setback, and evil are the repercussions. And to all who believe they cannot lose their salvation (eternal security), this is not a license to do whatever you want and just repent. Hebrews 6:4-6 clearly states that those who choose to receive Christ and the Word of God are subject to judgment for disobeying any of God's commandments.

Proverbs teach the principle of 'the fear of the Lord is the beginning of wisdom' (Proverbs 1:7). Rejecting this principle leads to foolishness and pride. Paul urged believers to live in holiness (1

Thessalonians 4:3–4), sanctification (John 17:17), justification (Romans 5:1), and righteousness (Romans 5:19). When these principles are ignored, corruption grows. Modern examples include corporate greed, moral relativism, and lack of integrity in leadership.

Principles act as guardrails for life. When we honor them, we stay on the path of wisdom and blessing. When we ignore them, we veer into destruction. Disobedience of principles leads to suffering, but obedience brings life and peace.

Chapter 4:

The Disobedience of Marriage

Marriage is a covenant designed by God to reflect His love, unity, and faithfulness. It is a sacred union between a man and a woman, intended for companionship, fruitfulness, and spiritual growth. Disobedience within marriage undermines this divine design and leads to brokenness. Disobedience and disrespect also violate the biblical order and create tension within the marriage. Disobeying the command against adultery led to broken families, distrust, and societal collapse.

God is a God of order, and a marriage out of order is not a godly marriage. Christ is the head of every marriage, next is the husband, then the wife and finally the children. Any woman who decides and believes that her children come before her husband is out of order. However, some men are not worthy of this honor, but God makes the rules. Arguments, hurtful words, abuse, dishonor, frustration, blessings, unanswered prayers, and many other things that come between the two becoming one flesh are the consequences of disobedience in the order of marriage.

God created marriage in Genesis 2:23-24, declaring, "And Adam said, This is now bone of my bones, and flesh of my flesh: she shall be called Woman, because she was taken out of Man. A man shall leave his father and mother and be joined to his wife, and they shall become one flesh." This union was designed to be permanent and faithful. Furthermore, to become one flesh is physical and spiritual, meaning nothing can be divided, nothing in between, and nothing outside can interfere. In essence, everything of him becomes her, and everything of her becomes him. If he hurts, she hurts; if she rejoices, he rejoices; his DNA becomes her DNA. Ultimately, no more "me life", time to start doing Us. Yet, disobedience has crept into marriage in many forms: adultery, neglect, abuse, and abandonment.

First, let us journey through our heart's choices of neglect. The Bible stated that the two shall become one flesh. To neglect your spouse is to neglect yourself, and when we neglect ourselves, we are neglecting God and Jesus, who dwells in us. Neglect comes in many forms, such as communication, physical affection and intimacy, responsibilities, nurturing, protection, emotional comfort, and spiritual fellowship. Neglect is defined as the failure to properly care for someone or something, or the state of being uncared for. This is a grave mistake to neglect God's commands to love and respect one another. When spouses neglect these responsibilities, marriages grow cold, resentful, and fragile.

In 1 Corinthians 7: 3-4, Let the husband render unto the wife due benevolence: and likewise also the wife unto the husband. The wife hath not power of her own body, but the husband: and likewise also the husband hath not power of his own body, but the wife. Disobeying and neglecting your spouse results in disobedience regardless of the circumstances. Nevertheless, if mutual consent is compromised, both can rejoice. Consequently, the neglect often leads to affairs, pornography addiction, pedophilia and other sexual misconduct. Everyone has their own choice; however, do not let this type of neglect cause your spouse to stumble. Many prayers have been hindered, and other family issues have arisen because of this disobedience. God knows everything, and He is watching closely!

Unfortunately, abuse is probably the most destructive disobedience a marriage can encounter. As with neglect, abuse comes in many forms but destroys the inner nature of the spouse. Abuse can rise in mental, physical, emotional, spiritual and financial. Often, marital abuse stems from a misconception of roles and order. For instance, ever since the feminist movement, women's equality, and women wanting to do jobs that were dominantly male, we have embraced a power struggle in relationships. Notably, this is not God's order.

Mental, physical, and emotional abuse is also birth from alcohol, drugs, and any other mind-stimulating disorder. Thus, it should never be tolerated, and one must seek help as soon as possible. The disobedience of abuse in marriage causes mental breakdowns, suicides, physical harm, and emotional heartaches that lead to severe health problems such as cardiovascular issues. In Ephesians 5:22-28, wives are commanded to submit themselves to their husbands, and husbands are to love their wives as Christ loved the church and gave Himself to it. The text in no way sounds like control or force, but conditionally upon love.

Furthermore, if the wife has to be submissive to her husband to receive unconditional love, just as we must be submissive to Christ to receive His love, we have to give to receive. Nevertheless, no woman should be submissive to an abusing, unloving man. That's like the blind leading the blind. Lastly, there is always room for repentance and a change of heart, but if the pattern persists, please get help.

Abuse, whether physical, emotional, or spiritual, is a grievous disobedience that distorts God's design for marriage. It violates the call to love, honor, and protect one another. The consequences include trauma, broken homes, and generational cycles of dysfunction. Many times, husbands are told to love their wives and not be bitter against them (Colossians 3:19). Bitterness, resentment, anger, aggressiveness, and poor life choices fuel abuse and before you realize it, atrocious behavior has manifested, and the outcome has resulted in a harmful altercation.

A preventive measure against abuse is found in Ephesians 4:29, 31-32. If our speech is always seasoned with grace and without any evil speaking nor malice, your marriage will be fruitful and your spouse will give of themselves freely, often and with joy unspeakable. Consistently, remember not only does abuse affect the spouse but also the children and close loved ones.

"It hath been said, Whosoever shall put away his wife, let him give her a writing of divorcement: But I say unto you, That whosoever shall put away his wife, saving for the cause of fornication, causeth her to commit adultery: and whosoever shall marry her that is divorced committeth adultery (Matthew 5:31-32)." Abandonment is a cowardly cop-out of the vows, responsibilities, and promises that were shared through intimacy. Once you have signed up for the position, it's time for the long haul. And if you venture to say the marriage was a mistake from the beginning, what stopped you from thinking and praying for divine discernment?

Because your spouse is not the person you thought you were marrying, is not behaving the way you think they should, or things are not going the way you expected, that is not a reason to abandon them and just give up. On all occasions, remember to return to the first love, what attracted both of you and the desire set forth at the start. To run is to dishonor God and your spouse. Therefore, what God has joined together, let no one separate." – Matthew 19:6

In 1 Corinthians 7:12-16, we find an exception regarding an unbelieving spouse. Although the text states, "if the unbelieving spouse wants to depart, let him depart still does not give the right to abandon the spouse. At least be respectful and upfront about your departure. "He who finds a wife finds what is good and receives favor from the Lord." (Proverbs 18:22). Let every man make that his quest for obedience. In a world that promotes, "If you're not happy, move on and find what makes you happy," that's not the order of God. Abandoning a spouse and, often, children as well is detrimental to the health and well-being of your family.

Adultery is one of the most destructive forms of disobedience in marriage. It violates trust, shatters intimacy, and often leads to divorce. Proverbs 6:32 warns, "The one who commits adultery has no sense; whoever does so destroys himself." The consequences extend beyond the couple to children, families, and society.

Adultery is one of the stupidest choices a person can make part in. God clearly says in the seventh commandment, "Thou shalt not commit adultery (Exodus 20:14). The consequence is death. Modern society today thinks it's okay, and because judgment is not speedy, it can be done repeatedly. A stern warning: the disobedience in committing adultery may not bring the sentence upon you, but it will come to your children or grandchildren. God takes marriage to heart, and unfaithfulness is hatred to Him.

For all that is in the world, the lust of the flesh, and the lust of the eyes, and the pride of life, is not of the Father, but is of the world. And the world passeth away, and the lust thereof: but he that doeth the will of God abideth for ever (1 John 2:16-17). Do not be led by temptation and overcome by lust, which pleasures for a moment. But be captivated by true love from God the Father, who will convey love in you and through you to your spouse.

Divorce, though permitted in cases of unfaithfulness, was never God's original design. Disobedience to this covenant leads to fractured families, emotional scars, and societal instability. A lot of marriages have ended in tragic financial settlements, child custody battles, and a life of heartache.

Yet, obedience within marriage produces blessing. Couples who honor God's design experience intimacy, partnership, and joy. Their marriage becomes a testimony of God's faithfulness and love.

The lesson is clear: disobedience in marriage destroys, but obedience builds a strong and lasting covenant.

God designed marriage as a covenant (Genesis 2:24). Adultery violates this covenant (Exodus 20:14), as seen in David's sin with Bathsheba (2 Samuel 11). Neglect and abuse also destroy marriages, leaving scars on families and children. Today, high divorce rates and rising infidelity illustrate society's disregard for God's design. Couples who live in obedience, however, reflect Christ's love for the Church (Ephesians 5:25–33).

CHAPTER 5:

THE DISOBEDIENCE OF CHILDREN

Children are commanded to obey their parents in the Lord, for "this is right" (Ephesians 6:1). Disobedience to parents is not only rebellion against family authority but also rebellion against God's order. Furthermore, children are inherently disobedient from birth, and scripture declares to "Train up a child in the way he should go: and when he is old, he will not depart from it (Proverbs 22:6)."

God commands children to honor their parents. To disobey this commandment is to disobey God, who is the Father of all. In addition, this command was given with the promise of a long life. Even if the child feels or believes that their parent(s) are not deserving of honor, still do your best to honor them regardless of the situation. Ultimately, the development of children's personality traits, respect for others, and overall contribution to society stems from honoring parents.

In the Old Testament, disobedience to parents was treated with utmost seriousness. Deuteronomy 21:18–21 prescribes severe consequences for rebellious sons who refuse to heed correction. This shows how seriously God views dishonor within the family. The passages may present a harsh judgment resulting in the child being stoned to death; nevertheless, if children have no regard for their parents, more than likely they will have no respect for anyone else.

Furthermore, if the parent decides to spare the rod and not discipline the child (Proverbs 13:24), the consequences of early incarceration, taking one's own life or destructive behavior will be their demise.

Today, children's disobedience manifests as rebellion, disrespect, and disregard for authority. This often leads to strained family relationships, educational struggles, and poor life choices. Societies with widespread youth rebellion experienced increased crime, violence, and instability. A total of 435 active shooter incidents in schools across the United States have occurred since 1999. That's not counting the number of deaths, injuries and suicides. There is definitely a disobedience problem among children worldwide, and the only cure is obedience and a righteous upbringing.

The consequences of disobedience for children can be long-lasting. Proverbs 30:17 warns, "The eye that mocks a father, that scorns an aged mother, will be pecked out by the ravens." While this is poetic imagery, it underscores the seriousness of dishonoring parents. It also unveils the frequent loss of temper and challenging authority, which sometimes results in children killing their parents.

"Wherein in time past ye walked according to the course of this world, according to the prince of the power of the air, the spirit that now worketh in the children of disobedience: Among whom also we all had our conversation in times past in the lusts of our flesh, fulfilling the desires of the flesh and of the mind; and were by nature the children of wrath, even as others (Ephesians 2:2-3)." The world, social media, video games and other things ruled by the prince of the power of the air are stealing the youth, development, and nature of our children.

Obedience to parents, however, brings blessings. Ephesians 6:2–3 promises, "Honor your father and mother"—which is the first commandment with a promise— "so that it may go well with you and that you may enjoy long life on the earth."

Obedient children grow into responsible, respectful adults who contribute positively to society. Children who display disobedience to parents often suffer from emotional and mental abuse, while trying to find love in the wrong people or harmful vices (drugs, alcohol, etc.).

The family is the foundation of society, and children's disobedience undermines that foundation. But when children obey, families thrive, and society is strengthened.

The children are reflections of their parents, and the parents are reflections of God. When families are functioning well, society can be fruitful, but when disobedience is present, so is malfunction and tragedy.

Children are commanded to obey their parents (Ephesians 6:1–3). Disobedience dishonors family order and invites consequences. The

Old Testament warned of severe penalties for rebellious children (Deuteronomy 21:18–21).

Today, youth rebellion often leads to crime, broken education, and fractured societies. Conversely, children who honor their parents often prosper in life and build stable families.

CHAPTER 6:

THE DISOBEDIENCE OF SOCIETY

Societies are built on shared values, laws, and principles. When a society collectively disobeys God's truth, it invites corruption, injustice, and collapse. History is filled with examples of civilizations that fell because of widespread disobedience. Woodrow Wilson once said: "A nation which does not remember what it was yesterday, does not know what it is today, nor what it is trying to do. We are trying to do a futile thing if we do not know where we came from or what we have been about."

"Never in the history of mankind have so many lived so freely, so rightfully, so humanely. This open democratic republic is man's highest achievement—not only for what it has already accomplished, but more importantly because it affords the greatest opportunity for orderly change and the realization of man's self-renewing aspirations. Our goals, as set forth in the Declaration, have been buttressed by a Constitution, a system of checks and balances, and mechanisms judicial, legislative, and executive that permit the continuation of Western civilization's spirited dialogue. This unhampered dialogue makes possible the opportunity to continuously approximate, through our legislative and judicial system, our moral and spiritual goals (Liebman, 1992)."

The world today is so far worse off than in 1992. Although freely, yet it is plagued by violence, hatred, abuse, neglect, coveting, and many other evils. Unfortunately, the legislative and judicial systems are not functioning as they did back in 1992. Societal morals and spiritual goals have taken a detour from the godly order of the Bible.

The generation of Noah illustrates this vividly. Genesis 6:5 says, "The Lord saw how great the wickedness of the human race had become on the earth." Society had become so corrupt that God sent the flood to cleanse the earth. God may never send a flood again; conversely, the disobedience in society today will bring severe judgment. It was said on a social media platform that if God is real, ask Him to end and heal childhood cancer. God is able to do just that. However, in response to the request, are societies able to be obedient to His Word? God is a covenant promise keeping Father, "Therefore thou shalt love the Lord thy God, and keep his charge, and his statutes, and his judgments, and his commandments, always (Deuteronomy 11:1)." The eleventh chapter of Deuteronomy expresses God's promises of no diseases, famine, baren women, provision and His goodness, but the contingent is obedience.

Sodom and Gomorrah also illustrate societal disobedience, where unchecked sin led to fiery judgment. This story presented a solemn warning against homosexuality and same sex marriages. For a man to declare he is a woman and a woman changing her nature to be a man is wickedness and an abomination to God. Did God make a mistake in creating those who believe they were born the opposite sex, certainly not? Everything in life is derived from heart choices. That's why a heart not fully committed to Jesus is "deceitful above all things, and desperately wicked: who can know it (Jeremiah 17:9)? The societal disobedience of same sex relationships has brought God's wrath on humanity (Romans 1:18, 24, 26-32).

The Israelites on the journey from Egypt to the Promised Land were a society of over 600,000 people. They grew greater throughout the journey, and so did their disobedience. From idolatry, wanting a king other than God, forsaking the commandments and the Sabbath. Notably, any wickedness or disobedience was not permitted in the camp. The individual who committed the disobedience was put outside the camp to be made clean or stoned to death. God has been very merciful and gracious toward society's disobedience, and we shall be thankful for His patience.

In the previous chapter, over four hundred school shootings have occurred, and that does not include the mass shootings at malls, grocery stores and other public venues. Societal disobedience has caused much fear, leading people to be afraid to go out in public. Corruption, unethical behavior, indiscipline, and uncontrolled anger have led to an increase in violence and exploitation of the less fortunate. "Corruption undermines social cohesion and trust. When people believe the system is rigged in favor of the powerful and corrupt, they are less likely to participate in civic life or cooperate. This can lead to further social and political instability (NTF, 2023)."

But to the wicked God says: "What right have you to declare My statutes, Or take My covenant in your mouth, seeing you hate instruction and cast My words behind you (Psalm 50:16-17). All societies have been given instructions in how to function as a community of people living in the Word of God. Disobedience brings the hate that makes us rebel against Divine instructions. Not only is it a right but a privilege to declare God's statute because it displays our obedience and discipline, and love for God and fellow mankind. Furthermore, throughout history there has been a rise in population but a decline in society's growth. Social norms, moral character, and respect depend upon one's feelings and perspective.

When you saw a thief, you consented with him And have been a partaker with adulterers. You give your mouth to evil, And your tongue frames deceit (Psalm 50:18-19). The Bible also states that "Death and life are in the power of the tongue, And those who love it will eat its fruit (Proverbs 18:21). Shall we take heed in the power given to us to build, encourage, and strengthen the character and well-being of society, or do we continue in the dismantling of one another? It is truly sad to see how we have come to tolerate, accept and consent to the evil practices in our culture today. The really horrifying outlook is that things will get even worse.

"Now consider this, you who forget God, Lest I tear you in pieces, And there be none to deliver: Whoever offers praise glorifies Me; And to him who orders his conduct aright I will show the salvation of God (Psalm 50:22-23)." Opportunity still awaits us to turn from our wicked ways and turn to God and be obedient for the rest of our existence on earth. Praise be to God for not giving us what we deserve and being gracious and long-suffering.

In modern times, societies that reject God's principles experience moral decay, political corruption, and social unrest. When truth is discarded and sin is celebrated, the stability of nations is undermined. And the question that no one is seeking is, why do civilizations rise, flourish, and fall? How can we build anything sustainable if we are steadily destroying nature, the environment and one another? As mentioned before, God has given us everything that pertains to life and godliness (2 Peter 1:3). The United States of America was established on the principles of God's word; what happened to stir us toward the evil of following alternative religions while disregarding the foundation of our forefathers?

The Apostle Paul warned in Romans 1 that societies that reject God exchange truth for lies and righteousness for unrighteousness. The consequences are moral confusion, idolatry, and eventual judgment. As soon as our heart chooses to exchange the truth for lies, a dividing of good and evil prevails, and things such as intersectionality invade the minds and hearts of the people who have chosen the lies.

The latter part of Romans 1 can be perceived as a judgment on the wicked and unrighteous rascals. Furthermore, there seems to be a world of moral confusion, with celebrities as idols and increasingly wicked performances, videos, reels, and feed content.

Yet, obedience to God within society brings blessing. Proverbs 14:34 says, "Righteousness exalts a nation, but sin condemns any people." When societies honor God's principles, they experience justice, peace, and prosperity. The opposite of a blessing is a curse. In society today, there are fewer blessings than curses. Justice and peace come at the expense of a tragedy or loss of life.

Furthermore, prosperity is eaten up by greed and control. The average family doesn't exist, and the struggle to make ends meet is a daunting task for single parents and now single living. Is this another argument for why things happen to good people? Should God bless certain individuals because they are struggling, or has He provided everything we need, but our disobedience and the evil we commit have caused so much division and prevented us from coming together as the church in Acts 2?

Society's disobedience affects everyone, but obedience can also bring widespread blessing. Notably, we must understand and remember that sin entered the world because of disobedience, and now all of creation is affected by its horrifying grip and destructive ways. "God creates order, humans create disorder, so God works on a disordered world to turn it the right way up, and that is revolution (Focus on the Family)." Therefore, the choice is left to the individual: will he or she choose Jesus or the world? The book of Revelation is like a cruise ship in motion, and the prophecies are unfolding in societies today. Nevertheless, God is patiently waiting for many to repent, come to Jesus, and turn from disobedience.

When entire societies disobey God, the results are catastrophic. Noah's generation was destroyed in the flood (Genesis 6:5–7). Sodom and Gomorrah faced fire for their wickedness (Genesis 19:24–25). Paul warned that rejecting God leads societies to embrace lies and corruption (Romans 1:21–32). Modern examples include societies plagued by violence, corruption, and immorality. By contrast, nations that uphold justice and righteousness often prosper.

CHAPTER 7:

THE DISOBEDIENCE OF LOVE

Love is the greatest commandment. Love is not optional in the Christian life—it is central. Jesus declared in Matthew 22:37-39, "'Love the Lord your God with all your heart and with all your soul and with all your mind.' This is the first and greatest commandment. And the second is like it: 'Love your neighbor as yourself.' All the Law and the Prophets hang on these two commandments." According to Christ, love is the foundation on which every other commandment rests. When love fails, obedience collapses, because disobedience in love is, at its root, disobedience to God Himself. Disobedience in love is, therefore, one of the gravest failures.

When people fail to love God, their hearts drift toward idols. This idolatry may not always take the form of carved statues, but it manifests in devotion to material wealth, personal ambition, pleasure, or power. As Paul writes in Romans 1:25, "They exchanged the truth about God for a lie, and worshiped and served created things rather than the Creator." Such disobedience leaves a void, because created things can never satisfy the longing of the human soul. The result is spiritual emptiness, despair, and separation from God.

Disobedience in love also reveals itself in the way we treat others. John writes bluntly in 1 John 4:20, "Whoever claims to love God yet hates a brother or sister is a liar." When love for others is absent, hatred, violence, injustice, and division thrive. History testifies to this truth: wars fueled by hatred, slavery born of greed and dehumanization, and modern examples of racism, domestic abuse, and systemic oppression. Each of these is the bitter fruit of failing to obey the command of love. When people fail to love others, the result is hatred, violence, injustice, and division.

1 Corinthians 13 describes love as patient, kind, not self-seeking, not easily angered, and always persevering. Consequently, 1 Corinthians 13 is the definition of love and not what we think or perceive love to be or not to be. If a poll of 15 people on how we define love were taken, there would probably be 7-12 different responses. Thus shall not be. Our love may be expressed in different ways, but all should stem from 1 Corinthians 13. In fact, since God is love, our love should manifest from Him. Disobedience of this standard produces jealousy, pride, anger, and unforgiveness. All of which promote the evil of deception, manipulation, coveting and bearing false witnesses. The consequences are broken relationships, bitterness, and hostility.

"He who does not love does not know God, for God is love (1 John 4:8). God is known by love, and where there is no love, God does not dwell there. And we often ask why so much evil prevails and why God is allowing it? The disobedience and absence of godly love are dormant in the hearts and minds of His creation. To God be the glory that it is a faithful few still embracing and sharing the love of God. Matthew 24:12 declares, "And because lawlessness will abound, the love of many will grow cold." Disobedience is the culprit for love growing cold.

"No one has seen God at any time. If we love one another, God abides in us, and His love has been perfected in us (1 John 4:12)." Many believe that they can love God without loving the people they interact with. Nevertheless, the Bible says otherwise, and loving others is how love is perfected in us. It takes faith to love a God not tangibly seen, and it takes faith to love one another as well. Actually, God is seen in loving one another and pouring out the fruit of the Spirit. The individual is transformed into the image of God when love is manifested. The goal of the Christian is to abide in love every day, all day. If faith never stops and the just shall live by it, then love shall have the same principles.

"There is no fear in love; but perfect love casts out fear, because fear involves torment. But he who fears has not been made perfect in love (1 John 4:18)." Love requires vulnerability, which in some cases causes fear and anxiety. However, we must have the courage to love unconditionally and be perfected in love. Fear says to the individual, You're afraid to try, too nervous to embrace, and worried about the outcome of being hurt or abused. Furthermore, fear invites doubt, unbelief, and trust. The fearful often make excuses to avoid stepping out in faith and letting God perfect His love in and through them.

"Whoever believes that Jesus is the Christ is born of God, and everyone who loves Him who begot also loves him who is begotten of Him. 2 By this we know that we love the children of God, when we love God and keep His commandments. 3 For this is the love of God, that we keep His commandments. And His commandments are not burdensome (1 John 5:1-3)." Thou cannot love without obeying, and thou cannot obey without love. Some say love is hard and challenging; however, when love is unconditional, freely open, and just, it captivates and flows like a rushing river, embracing all within its path. Only disobedience makes the commandments burdensome.

Societies that disobey love are filled with violence, discrimination, and oppression. Families that disobey love experience conflict, division, and estrangement. Individuals who disobey love live with loneliness and bitterness. Oppression and violence have escalated through the centuries because of the lack of love and disobedience. Reporting of murders, religious persecution, economic inequality, dictatorship, community violence, state-sanctioned violence and terrorism are the forces that suppress love while influencing hate. The evil one has been dividing the family and causing conflict since the beginning. He knows that a family filled with the love of God and love for one another will be fruitful and last forever. Bitterness chokes away love and leaves the individual in a state of depression, suicide, and despondency.

Yet, obedience in love produces blessing. Love restores, heals, and unites. It reflects the very nature of God, for "God is love" (1 John 4:8). The cross of Christ is the ultimate demonstration of love's obedience, where Jesus gave His life for sinners. In addition, "above all things have fervent love for one another, for "love will cover a multitude of sins (1 Peter 4:8)." Our love has the power to cover the sins of our loved ones, those who have fallen away and returned to Jesus, and even the unsaved. Jesus says to the church in Ephesus "you have left your first love." Thus, should not be, if thou hast left the first love which is Jesus, please repent and ask to be restored immediately.

Disobedience of love destroys, but obedience in love transforms lives, families, and societies. We are in desperate need of a transformation in all three of these entities. Love is more powerful than we can imagine.

Love formed the world, created humanity and creatures, and connected us to one another to live in harmony and on one accord. Love, in its unconditional and agape state, transforms the heart of stone into the loving nature of God.

Love says to one another, "I care for your well-being and to see you prosper in health and life. Let us no longer continue in disobedience and destroying one another and the earth. God richly bless us to enjoy!

Jesus said the greatest commandments are to love God and love others (Matthew 22:37–39). Paul described love's qualities in 1 Corinthians 13. When love is absent, hatred, violence, and unforgiveness thrive. Today, rising domestic violence, racial tension, and division show the fruit of disobedience of love. Obedience in love restores peace, unity, and healing.

CHAPTER 8:

THE DISOBEDIENCE OF LEADERSHIP

Leadership carries great responsibility. Leaders influence nations, organizations, and communities. "Disobedience in leadership can have significant consequences, both spiritually and practically. Leaders who disobey God's instructions risk divine rejection and the loss of spiritual backing. Disobedience can also lead to partial obedience being viewed as total disobedience, as God values complete compliance above selective compliance. Additionally, disobedience can result in spiritual blindness and self-deception, where leaders lose the ability to discern the truth about themselves (Rev. Samuel Arimoro)." When leaders disobey God, the consequences ripple through those they lead.

"Leadership in God's kingdom carries great responsibility. It is a sacred trust, not a personal entitlement. When leaders obey God, they become channels of blessing and direction. But when they disobey, they bring confusion, judgment, and reproach upon themselves and the people they lead. The higher the calling, the heavier the consequences of rebellion (Rev. Samuel Arimoro)."

Leaders are not exempt from disobedience, and everyone under their authority will be affected, including family members. Church leaders, CEOs and other people of authority often do not think about their disobedience because, as Ecclesiastes 8:11 states, "Because sentence against an evil work is not executed speedily, therefore the heart of the sons of men is fully set in them to do evil." How many of us really think about the consequences for every word spoken, deed done, and action and behavior performed? Another important thing to remember is that the consequences may not be placed upon you, but on your children or even your grandchildren.

Saul, Israel's first king, disobeyed God and lost his kingdom. His pride, impatience, and fear of people brought destruction upon Israel. David's disobedience brought turmoil to his household and nation. The Bible conveys many kings who disobeyed God and did what was evil in His sight. The intriguing fact is how many years these evil kings ruled. They often ruled for decades and caused destruction and chaos among the people of God. A striking lesson to take heed of is that when the people did evil, He allowed these kings to rule over them. Therefore, when a selfish, unrighteous leader is placed in a position of power, the people should take heed of their disobedience and repent, and God will remove them.

"Leaders must carefully consider the consequences of their actions, whether they choose to challenge or disobey orders from higher authorities. It is crucial to align personal values with organizational values and to communicate concerns to superiors when necessary (Doug Thorpe)." Many leaders challenge the authority of Jesus without knowing or caring about the consequences. Jesus says in Luke 6:46, "But why do you call Me 'Lord, Lord,' and not do the things which I say? One day, the leaders will have to give an account for every word and deed not followed. And they should know that this is disobedience to Jesus's leadership. Furthermore, our values have to align with God's standards and values.

Modern history is filled with leaders whose corruption, greed, or immorality led nations into war, poverty, and collapse. History has been a lesson in the corruption of the leaders of nations, organizations, governments, communities, and families. The unfortunate value that is lost is that the individual usually starts out sincere, ethical, and passionate. The saying goes, "If you want to find out the true heart of a person, give them power or money." With all the resources, millionaires, and billionaires, can poverty truly be better managed? Leaders are supposed to delegate and put people in the right position to avoid collapse and strengthen one another. Disobedience in leadership results in oppression, injustice, and suffering for the people.

Leadership in the family structure has been devastated by missing fathers in the home, Christ not welcomed in the home, and a lack of respect and love within the unity of the family. According to the U.S. Census Bureau, in 2020, 24.7 million children (33%) in the United States lived in fatherless homes. This number has increased by 25% since 1960 (Colin Tan). These alarming statistic stems from divorce, abandonment, incarceration, separation, and unmarried couples. The broken order has caused disobedience in leadership that sometimes never develops. Meaning, some men are not taught by God and their father on how to be a good father.

Many will argue that there are many homes with fathers who do not believe in Jesus and don't go to church, and will say they are doing well. Nevertheless, they may do well for a season, but without God, some type of issue will arise. Furthermore, without Jesus, who sets the standards and principles? Standards and principles only come from two sources: the world or God. To all men without a father or wise man in your life, please, with urgency, seek Jesus and let God guide you in becoming the best man He created you to be. It is time for all men to stop being disobedient in their call to leadership and show, not "prove" to all you encounter that you are a leader your who needs to be respected and love.

Jesus taught that true leadership is servanthood: "Whoever wants to become great among you must be your servant" (Mark 10:43). Disobedience to this principle leads to prideful, self-serving leadership. Leaders in the church have misused servanthood in thinking they are supposed to be served. When a fellowship event is going on, many leaders have the best seats in the place while being served first. Jesus said he came to serve, not to be served. Are we greater than He? To all who are called to leadership, Jesus should be your example, model, and mentor. Unfortunately, there are people who take on leadership roles because of higher pay or because no one else is available to fill the position. This also results in disobedience in leadership. The bible declares, "Many are called, but a few are chosen." If you're not chosen for leadership, please do yourself a huge favor and don't take the position. There is nothing wrong with being part of the multitude. We are all important together, from the least to the greatest.

The consequences are clear: disobedient leaders bring destruction, but obedient leaders bring blessings. When leaders honor God, they guide people with wisdom, integrity, and justice. The lack of integrity has been a major cause of leadership disobedience, and it seems that, over time, integrity is increasingly absent. Leadership, in itself, is supposed to produce wise leaders and wise counsel. Many leaders in the Bible caused destruction and death to many women, children and men. However, there were a few that we can learn from and become wise and great leaders.

Leadership carries accountability before God. Saul's pride cost him his kingdom (1 Samuel 15). David's census brought plague on Israel (2 Samuel 24:10–15). Today, corrupt leaders cause wars, oppression, and poverty. Jesus modeled servant leadership (Mark 10:43–45), teaching that leaders must serve. Obedient leaders uplift nations, while disobedient ones destroy them.

CHAPTER 9:

THE DISOBEDIENCE OF NATIONS

Nations are held accountable before God. The Old Testament is filled with examples of nations judged for their disobedience. Egypt, Babylon, Assyria, and others rose to power but fell into ruin because of pride and rebellion. Sodom and Gomorrah were destroyed for their wickedness (Genesis 19). Israel itself, chosen by God, was exiled to Babylon because of persistent disobedience (2 Chronicles 36:15–21). Yet when nations repented, God relented.

"And nation was destroyed of nation, and city of city: for God did vex them with all adversity (2 Chronicles 15:6)." This verse conveys the turmoil caused when nations disobey God's ways. Instead of coming together as one nation under God indivisible, with liberty and justice for all, we are in competition with one another, destroying others' reputations, and committing all types of corruption. "By observing the afflictions faced by nations, we are called to reflect on our actions and relationship with God. It is a sobering reminder that neglecting God, whether by indulging in immorality or turning away from His teachings, leads to chaos and strife not only personally but also corporately within societies (Pastor David)."

When a nation disobeys God by embracing idolatry, injustice, and immorality, it invites judgment. The results of these behaviors lead to divine judgment, disciplining the nation, and, unfortunately, many innocents are caught in the crossfire. We must always remember that sin entered the entire world, not just those who choose to commit it. Proverbs 14:34 reminds us, "Righteousness exalts a nation, but sin condemns any people." It would be a blessing for all nations to be exalted; however, too many have been overtaken by the evil one and following after other gods. Romans 8:1 tells us, "There is therefore now no condemnation to them which are in Christ Jesus, who walk not after the flesh, but after the Spirit." If we sin, then we should be condemned.

Seeing that Abraham shall surely become a great and mighty nation, and all the nations of the earth shall be blessed in him (Genesis 18:8). What has led us from this promise of blessings to the destruction we are living in today? History has taught us that the fall of man is steadily increasing over time. Each decade, century, and millennium, we are more disobedient, more corrupt, and more immoral. Abraham was a righteous man who displayed faith in God, which manifested in a mighty nation. Woefully, the nations that followed became unrighteous, disobedient, and sinful.

A nation is conventionally more overtly political than ethnically. It is a shame that only in America are people classified and categorized. For instance, African American is the title for black people, Asian Americans are said to be yellow; nevertheless, in other countries, people are European, Brazilian, Chinese and not an African European or Asian Brazilian. Consequently, this is where division arises, and the separation of God's creativity, ethical, and moral standards is trampled on, and nations despise one another.

According to Wikipedia, the United Nations (UN) is a global intergovernmental organization established by the signing of the UN Charter on 26 June 1945 with the articulated mission of maintaining international peace and security, to develop friendly relations among states, to promote international cooperation, and to serve as a centre for harmonizing the actions of states in achieving those goals. Together, 193 sovereign states make up the United Nations, and they meet annually to discuss global and political issues that could disrupt peace. It's ironic that how over half a century, they have not attempted to solve issues of violence, poverty, and healthier living conditions. Neglect is a form of disobedience if we are told to "love our neighbor." The consequences of our actions stem from neglecting world problems and from not coming together to seek God for resolutions.

"And I will shake all nations, and the desire of all nations shall come: and I will fill this house with glory, saith the Lord of hosts (Haggai 2:7)." This Scripture addresses biblical prophecy, and the desire of all nations is Jesus Christ Who is the needs of humanity and the only One that can offer wisdom, solutions, and love for all even if we are unenlightened. A general shaking did occur around the building site of the second temple (Ezra 1:1-4). As Matthew Henry stated in his concise commentary, "convulsions and changes would take place in the Jewish church and state, but first should come great revolutions and commotions among the nations." If all the nations of the world set Jesus Christ as the desire of all nations, the longing for God may be embraced from the Prince of Peace.

Modern nations that disregard God's principles face similar consequences: corruption, division, economic collapse, and loss of freedom. If we are aware of similar consequences, it should be a warning to change from disobedience to obedience to God's principles. Nations that exalt sin over righteousness cannot stand forever. Sin is very reckless and has no mercy on the nations that partake in its destruction, which brings death. Moreover, to exalt sin is to rebel against God's ethical and moral standards and laws. We are told to be "holy as God is holy, and to be perfect as God is perfect." These righteous actions can only be achieved through obedience to the word of God.

Yet, when nations turn to God, blessings flow. Nineveh repented at Jonah's preaching and was spared judgment. For it is written, "the Lord is not slack concerning his promise, as some men count slackness; but is longsuffering to us-ward, not willing that any should perish, but that all should come to repentance (2 Peter 3:9)." Nations that honor God's Word experience peace and prosperity. Although it is prophesied that lawlessness will increase, the evil one will deceive many, and nations will experience pain and suffering, there is still time to turn to God and be reconciled and saved through eternal life in Christ Jesus.

The fate of nations is tied to their obedience or disobedience. "Blessed and holy is he that hath part in the first resurrection: on such the second death hath no power, but they shall be priests of God and of Christ and shall reign with him a thousand years. And when the thousand years are expired, Satan shall be loosed out of his prison and shall go out to deceive the nations which are in the four quarters of the earth, Gog, and Magog, to gather them together to battle: the number of whom is as the sand of the sea (Revelation 20:6-8)." The mark of the beast and great tribulation will come, and those who obey Jesus will reign with Him, and Satan will deceive those who choose to be disobedient.

Nations that turn from God invite judgment. Babylon, Assyria, and Egypt all fell because of pride and rebellion (Isaiah 13; Nahum 1). Nineveh repented at Jonah's preaching and was spared (Jonah 3:10). Modern nations that legalize immorality or embrace corruption face division and decline. Nations should realize that we are all in this world together and that every choice we make, whether good or evil, affects us all. Proverbs 14:34 declares, 'Righteousness exalts a nation, but sin condemns any people.'

CHAPTER 10:

THE DISOBEDIENCE OF WORSHIP

Worship is meant to honor God, but disobedience can corrupt worship. When worship becomes about self, ritual, or idolatry, it loses its power and meaning. Worship is a lifestyle that should be practiced every day. If everything we do is to glorify God and bring glory to His name, worship must be at the forefront. Worship conveys to God that we honor Him, His commandments, and serving Him brings joy to our hearts. Worship aligns us with the Word of God, the call of God, and the praises of God. In addition, worship engages us in all aspects of our lives and serves as a purpose and a source of fulfillment in our spiritual growth. Worship transforms the heart by fostering a deeper relationship with the Divine Creator.

"But if thine heart turn away, so that thou wilt not hear, but shalt be drawn away, and worship other gods, and serve them (Deuteronomy 30:17)." In the world today, there are many other gods; other religions claim to be the true god. Even Christians have turned away from the Lord God to serve and worship other gods. Unfortunately, because it does not seem to appear that God's anger has been fury and no wrath or judgment has taken place, many are being deceived following after other gods that are dead, false doctrine, and no truth. Nevertheless, a movement of God's Holy Spirit is transforming the hearts of many Muslims, and they are accepting Jesus as their Savior and Lord.

Another sad disobedience of worship is the idolatry of celebrities. It is truly heartbreaking to see people worshipping celebrities and making them their idols. God is a jealous God, and on the day of judgment many will be disappointed by His judgment because they did not take heed to His voice in the Word of God (Bible). These celebrities are practicing wickedness, witchcraft, demonic ceremonies, and other abominable things. Furthermore, secular music mostly encourages violence, sexuality, and other negative behaviors. The entertainment industry loves to mention God's name in blessing them to the platform they currently possess; however, they fail to follow Him, worship Him and keep His commandments.

Israel often fell into disobedience in worship. They built golden calves, offered sacrifices to idols, and turned the temple into a marketplace. For thou shalt worship no other god: for the Lord, whose name is Jealous, is a jealous God. The Israelites often fell into the worship of Baal, causing God's anger to be aroused. Furthermore, they worshipped the goddess Ashtoreth, whose cult included fertility rituals, sex and love, and war. The sacrifices of children, burning incense, and other pagan rituals led Israel into captivity and the loss of many lives. In modern times, we may not be sacrificing children, but many Christians are practicing pagan rituals and holidays (Christmas, Easter, etc.).

"And they stood up in their place, and read in the book of the law of the Lord their God one fourth part of the day; and another fourth part they confessed, and worshipped the Lord their God (Nehemiah 9:3)." All nations of the earth should come together and perform this great assembly before the Almighty God. Worship ushers us into confession, repentance, forgiveness, and restoration. It is in worship that God's heart is open to receive us, love us, and bless us. We all worship something, whether it be money, fame, substance, status, people or self. Worshipping God in a daily routine takes away self and puts God at the top of our list. The Bible states, "No one can serve two masters" (Matthew 6:24). It is impossible to worship God and anything else. The choice is one or the other.

"All the earth shall worship thee, and shall sing unto thee; they shall sing to thy name (Psalm 66:4)." To come in the house of the Lord to sing praises and worship God on Sabbath or Sunday and the rest of the week is less knowledge of God, no singing praise, no prayer, no reading and listening to the Bible is hypocrisy. God is not a God of a two-hour service, and worship is more than singing a few songs. Acknowledging God every morning when you wake and thanking Him every night before bed are great ways to worship Him with honor and glory. To worship God only when the feeling is enhanced is disobedience and a lack of asking for His Spirit. Only hypocrites practice disobedience to worship.

Jesus rebuked such worship, declaring that true worshippers must worship in spirit and truth (John 4:24). It is impossible to worship that which is not true, and we are told to "walk in the Spirit." Therefore, every step you take should be in the Spirit with "Jesus the truth." Sadly, many believe they know the truth but worship false gods, false doctrine, and unfaithful people. God is seeking those who will worship Him in spirit and in truth. On the other hand, many are tempted by Satan and worship the things promised and not the Creator God. A child of God should be able to recognize the Spirit of truth over the children of disobedience.

Disobedience in worship leads to hypocrisy, empty rituals, and false religion. The consequence is spiritual blindness and separation from God. There is a lot of spiritual blindness in the world today. The blind leading the blind, pagan rituals leaving people empty and poor, and people claiming to be Christian but acting and looking like the world. Worship is a lifestyle that shows that I am God's child, that I love God and keep His commandments, and that I worship Him in holiness and reverence. The child of God is a reflection of His image that says to the world I worship God in obedience, devotion, and discipline.

Obedience in worship, however, brings God's presence, power, and blessing. Worship rooted in obedience transforms hearts and glorifies God. Moreover, it expresses the highest praise, bringing worthiness and honor to His holy name. The Psalmist declared, "I will bless the Lord at all times: his praise shall continually be in my mouth. My soul shall make her boast in the Lord: the humble shall hear thereof, and be glad. O magnify the Lord with me, and let us exalt his name together (Psalm 34:1-3)." There is power in worship and praise to God the Father and the Lord Jesus Christ.

Israel often corrupted worship with idols and empty rituals (Isaiah 1:13–15). Jesus rebuked temple corruption (Matthew 21:12–13) and taught true worship is 'in spirit and truth' (John 4:24). Today, when worship becomes entertainment or self-focused, it loses its power. True obedience in worship brings God's presence and transformation.

CHAPTER 11:

THE DISOBEDIENCE OF FAITH

Faith is central to the Christian life. "Now faith is the substance of things hoped for, the evidence of things not seen (Hebrews 11:1)." No one really knows what may take place tomorrow, next week or next month, but we make plans, set schedules, and predict what we want to happen. It is disobedient not to lay your plans before God. He is the One who determines the length of life. If faith is the substance of things hoped for, the substance must be our trust and belief that what we are hoping for will manifest and come to pass. Furthermore, there should be evidence of things that are not directly observed or visible. In essence, God knows who really has faith and exercises that faith to receive what is hoped for.

"For we are saved by hope: but hope that is seen is not hope: for what a man seeth, why doth he yet hope for? But if we hope for that we see not, then do we with patience wait for it (Romans 8:24-25)?" The Bible says faith can move mountains; nevertheless, do we have the patience to wait for it? Hope often seems to fade away the longer it takes to manifest. We live in an instant give society where patience is like a sin. Even the children are behaving with no patience and no hope that greater things will happen or come. Hope is probably the principal thing that engages the believer's faith in these last times we live in.

"Therefore being justified by faith, we have peace with God through our Lord Jesus Christ: By whom also we have access by faith into this grace wherein we stand, and rejoice in hope of the glory of God. And not only so, but we glory in tribulations also: knowing that tribulation worketh patience; And patience, experience; and experience, hope (Romans 5:1-4)." It is disobedient not to stand and rejoice in the hope of the glory of God because there is a working being manifested in the believer for their spiritual maturity. We will all experience tribulations, and the greater the hope, the greater the patience and the greater the experience of God's love.

Many people claim to have faith, and when their faith is tested in the fiery furnace, they look to everyone else instead of God. They call their loved ones, the pastor, or people they believe are prayer warriors. Notably, God does anoint pastors to pray for people and "the effectual fervent prayer of a righteous man availeth much (James 5:16)." However, it is very imperative to have faith in God as well. It is also essential to associate with people of faith because their faith may benefit you when the evil one has caused your faith to be weak. An innumerable number of Christians have fallen asleep or have no life because they refuse to exercise their faith.

Hebrews 11:6 declares, "Without faith it is impossible to please God." Disobedience in faith is unbelief, doubt, and fear. In the Old Testament, the Israelites would bring offerings and sacrifices to please God; however, the sacrifice was to satisfy the sin committed. The only faith they had was that God would not perish them. Likewise, in the world today, we are not exercising our faith to please God but "doing what we believe is right in our own eyes." We have put our faith in money, security, people, materialism, and the evil acts of the evil one. So, what and who do you really put faith in?

"Even so faith, if it hath not works, is dead, being alone. Yea, a man may say, Thou hast faith, and I have works: shew me thy faith without thy works, and I will shew thee my faith by my works (James 2:17-18)." Ah, without a working faith, nothing else matters cause your hope will have no substance. Too many Christians believe that if they just pray, everything is good. That prayer in faith sometimes requires us to do our part. Just as Abraham, by faith, left his hometown and trusted God to lead him to a place he did not know. Likewise, Hebrews 11 tells of many by working faith trusted God and followed wherever He led them. The substance of faith is always working with God to complete His purpose.

Disobedience of this principle leads to fear, unbelief, and missed blessings. The Israelites who refused to enter the Promised Land because of fear missed out on God's promises. Numerous bad choices stem from fear and not having faith as small as a mustard seed. Furthermore, many times God has declared to not be afraid and to fear not. Fear puts faith in the trunk like a spare tire and only utilizes it when convenient. Unbelief is a detrimental harm to faith and will not only displease God but also loose power and deny Jesus. Each one of us can count the missed blessings, the joy and the peace that would have resulted in praising God, but fear came and led us astray.

Israel's refusal to enter the Promised Land because of fear illustrates disobedience of faith. They were supposed to be models to the rest of the world and all that followed. Consequently, missed out on God's promises because they did not trust Him and were afraid of their enemies. "What shall we then say to these things? If God be for us, who can be against us (Romans 8:31)?" Faith proclaims, "that I will stand with God no matter what happens to me and even if no one else will stand I will." "When Peter, was walking on water, began to sink, his doubt snatched his faith in Jesus so fast that he panicked. This was a great lesson in faith and in how disobedience can turn trusting in Jesus into doubting His voice.

Disobedience of faith leads to missed blessings, fear, and defeat. Obedience of faith brings victory, miracles, and life. God is still in the miracle-working business, and victory is always overcome by faith. There are also many Christian's living a defeated life with no hope in ever being made free. Being free from worry of cancer, diseases, poverty, violence, death, and other tribulations has caused them to give up on life and Jesus. It is very easy to get discouraged in the world today because the majority of news reports involve killing, child abuse, corruption, or a decline in moral and ethical behavior. Nevertheless, the Christian hope, faith, and love are rooted in God the Father and the Lord Jesus Christ.

Faith is not optional—it is the foundation of obedience. An obedient faith is a working faith that trusts in Jesus, who is life and our all in all! The Bible does declare that each person has been given a measure of faith (Romans 12:3) and also in 2 Thessalonians 3:2, "and that we may be delivered from unreasonable and wicked men: for all men have not faith." Therefore, faith can be living and active or dead and not exist at all. Disobedience and wickedness will always display a lack of faith, resulting in wondering, searching, and never coming to the knowledge of Christ and His love and forgiveness. We live in a hurting and dying world where faith and hope are diminishing by the day.

Without faith, it is impossible to please God (Hebrews 11:6). Israel disobeyed by refusing to enter Canaan out of fear (Numbers 14:1–4). Peter sank when he doubted (Matthew 14:29–31). Modern believers disobey faith when they trust in wealth, science, or self above God. Faith is obedience; unbelief leads to missed blessings.

CHAPTER 12:

THE DISOBEDIENCE OF TRUTH

Truth is essential to God's character. The truth in what we believe and read about God is a profound true allegory for the condition and development of human consciousness. When the conscious mind heeds the call of God, the heart takes root in seeking the truth of God, Jesus, and our existence. Truth opens the mind and heart to receive revelations about God's nature, His heart and His character. The Holy Spirit, which is the Spirit of truth, is sent to manifest the truths from Scripture. In addition, the more the believer seeks truth (Jesus), the more the heart of God is revealed and embraced. Disobedience to truth is embracing lies, deception, and falsehood.

"He is the Rock, his work is perfect: for all his ways are judgment: a God of truth and without iniquity, just and right is he (Deuteronomy 32:4)." In a world where deception and lies are common, the only truth we need is found in God, and He grants us discernment and wisdom to not be deceived. Philippians 1:6 states, "Being confident of this very thing, that he which hath begun a good work in you will perform it until the day of Jesus Christ." That's truth declaring a promise, and only disobedience can interrupt the process. What God says He will do, consider it done in love and in truth. Furthermore, there is no wrong in a just God. He is faithful forevermore.

"Sin and disobedience lay hold of truth, grasp it roughly, and will not let it be what it naturally is or say what it naturally says. In this way, the deliberate dynamic of unbelief is to suppress the truth, stifle truth and hold truth hostage (Nathan Millican)." Jesus declared, "I am the way, the truth, and the life" (John 14:6). Following Jesus and obeying His commandments suppresses sin, and disobedience does not exist. Many have left the truth for a lie and lost the way in the One that gives life and life more abundantly (John 10:10). "The disobedience of truth involves a complex interplay between obedience, authority, and individual conscience, often leading to significant personal and societal consequences (Copilot Search)."

Satan is the father of lies, and when people reject truth, they align with his schemes. The consequences are confusion, division, and destruction. "Satan works on human minds, leading them to think that there is wonderful knowledge to be gained apart from God. By deceptive reasoning, he led Adam and Eve to doubt God's word, and to supply its place with a theory that led to disobedience. And his sophistry is doing today what it did in Eden (EGW, COL 108.1)." Satan loves to present fashion, fame, and self-glory, but in the end, the lies unveil sin and deception. One of his main schemes is division because a house that is divided cannot stand or function divinely. Jesus also, in John 8, spoke to the Pharisees in proclaiming that there is no truth in Satan, and he was a murderer from the beginning. No one should ever listen to or follow a murderer.

John 8:32, And ye shall know the truth, and the truth shall make you free. Notice the verse did not say "set you free," but "make you free." Although some translations do say "set you free," there is a striking difference between being set free and being made free. Only truth can make one free. There is an inner working of God, Jesus, and the Holy Spirit, making liberation evident in the saint's well-being spirit. Furthermore, the truth makes us whole and living out the truth in Jesus Christ is joy unspeakable. To be set free is to be relieved or released from sin or something, but to be made free is to be renewed, restored, and regenerated in Jesus.

Societies that reject truth become unstable. Families that reject the truth fall apart. Individuals who reject truth live in deception. Societies in the quest for riches and wealth have rejected the ways of God and rely on false promises, misleading marketing campaigns, and other schemes that have crippled the stability of unity and support of one another. Families have fallen short and only come together when there is a death in the family. Satan has come in and caused division and gossip, and lies. Individuals who are not following Jesus and reading the Bible, praying and studying are being deceived by every wind of doctrine. Look around, and there is a church in every neighborhood, but the conversion of saints is empty pews. Many claim to know the truth, walk in the truth, and talk about the truth, yet they do not practice what they preach.

Obedience to truth brings freedom, as Jesus said: "If the Son therefore shall make you free, ye shall be free indeed." (John 8:36). In America, we enjoy our freedom; freedom of speech, freedom to bear arms, freedom to worship, however, in other countries this is not so because there is usually one religion, and many are persecuted for the truth in Jesus Christ. Let us always pray for those countries that need the truth of Jesus Christ, and that those who are obedient will be made free. God can liberate any country He wants to, nonetheless, the countries that are free are not standing in the gap and being the example and model God has called us to be. We used to pledge allegiance to one nation under God, not gods. Can we get back to our first Love?

Disobedience of truth enslaves, but obedience to truth liberates. "But now being made free from sin, and become servants to God, ye have your fruit unto holiness, and the end everlasting life (Romans 6:22)." We have all experienced that feeling of joy, happiness, freedom when the truth is embraced. When set free from something or someone that had you in bondage and captivity, the joy of freedom can feel refreshing, exhilarating, and breathtaking. "Howbeit when he, the Spirit of truth, is come, he will guide you into all truth: for he shall not speak of himself; but whatsoever he shall hear, that shall he speak: and he will shew you things to come (John 16:13)." Always allow oneself to be led by the Spirit of truth. One can never go wrong or be lied to by the Spirit.

Jesus is the Truth (John 14:6). Rejecting truth leads to bondage (Romans 1:25). Satan is the father of lies (John 8:44). Societies that abandon truth collapse under deception and confusion. Today, fake news, misinformation, and denial of God's Word reflect disobedience of truth. Obedience to truth sets people free (John 8:32).

CHAPTER 13:

THE DISOBEDIENCE OF INTEGRITY

Integrity is living in honesty and consistency. Proverbs 10:9 says, "Whoever walks in integrity walks securely, but whoever takes crooked paths will be found out." "Then Peter and the other apostles answered and said, We ought to obey God rather than men (Acts 5:29)." The Apostles were told not to teach in the name of Jesus. There will come a time when we are faced with obeying God rather than man or civil laws, such as the soon-coming Sunday law. This law states that Sabbath keepers are to worship on Sunday, not Saturday. Nowhere in the Bible do we find Sunday as a holy day or the change of the Sabbath to Sunday. Those who keep the commandments of God will have their integrity tested. Disobedience will display no integrity at all, and you fear man rather than God.

The three Hebrew boys in Daniel 3 refused to bow down to the golden image of King Nebuchadnezzar and maintained their integrity, serving and bowing only to the King of kings and Lord of lords. They declared, "If it be so, our God whom we serve is able to deliver us from the burning fiery furnace, and he will deliver us out of thine hand, O king. But if not, be it known unto thee, O king, that we will not serve thy gods, nor worship the golden image which thou hast set up (Daniel 3:17-18)." In the king's fury, he had them put in a fiery furnace to be killed. Nevertheless, because of their integrity, Jesus showed up in the furnace and walked them through without any burns or smoke. Take heed that the Christian's integrity will always be challenged by the evil one and his minions.

The integrity of the mere Christian in today's society has been compromised by false acts of love (love sin, Jesus does), tolerating ungodly behavior, and compromising with abominations. This disobedience to our integrity has led to childhood cancer, breast cancer, poverty, unfaithfulness, and other moral declining health issues. Furthermore, news, television, entertainment, movies, and other venues promote violence, negative behaviors, horror, deception, and manipulation, all in the name of fun. Integrity is exhibited from within an individual; if someone else causes you to lose your integrity, that means that person has control over you. The lack of integrity has silenced the church from speaking boldly about the gospel of Jesus Christ, and false prophets preach about one another rather than Christ.

Job was a man of integrity, and his story in the Bible speaks thunderously about his relationship with and response to God in the midst of tragedy and loss. His children were taken from him by death, his livestock and servants were burned up, and Satan vexed him with sore boils, but in all of this, Job kept his integrity and "then Job arose, and rent his mantle, and shaved his head, and fell down upon the ground, and worshipped (Job 1:20), and proclaimed "What? Shall we receive good at the hand of God, and shall we not receive evil? In all this, did not Job sin with his lips (Job 2:10)?" No matter what happens to us, we must hold fast to our integrity because God is counting on us, and others are watching to see how we function in the midst of tribulations. Notably, it was God who allowed this to happen to Job.

Disobedience of integrity manifests as dishonesty, hypocrisy, and corruption. Leaders who lack integrity lead nations into ruin. Individuals who lack integrity destroy their reputations and relationships. The consequences of the disobedience of integrity are mistrust, shame, and downfall. Obedience to integrity brings security, trust, and honor. We will be judged for every word and deed done with integrity or not with integrity, and at the end of the day, we can only blame ourselves. The Bible leaves us with no excuses, and we should not excuse ourselves or blame others either. Honesty and uprightness should always be in our character, even when no one is watching but God. Integrity is one of the most valuable lessons a parent can teach their children and siblings.

"The integrity of the upright shall guide them: but the perverseness of transgressors shall destroy them (Proverbs 11:3)." Integrity is not taught or talked about in our social circles, and that is why we see so much perverseness. Transgression is a popular behavior among people, businesses, and communities. It has become so easy to lie, tell a white lie or just simply disobey. Integrity should be a foundational principle in walking in the Spirit and representing Jesus. Jesus is the Lord of integrity, and if we are in His likeness and image, we are to reflect the same image. "Judge me, O Lord; for I have walked in mine integrity: I have trusted also in the Lord; therefore I shall not slide (Psalm 26:1). Integrity will keep us in the ways and statutes of God.

Integrity is essential for life, leadership, and faith. Leadership without integrity is like many of the kings in the Old Testament, who did what was evil in the sight of God. The ability to motivate, influence, and lead into the righteousness of God failed because of a lack of faith, reverence, and integrity of heart. Integrity conveys that a saint will stand firm in the armor of God and not swayed or moved from His presence and commandments. Furthermore, "for though we walk in the flesh, we do not war after the flesh: (For the weapons of our warfare are not carnal, but mighty through God to the pulling down of strong holds (2 Corinthians 10:3-4)." Our integrity should be rooted in the Spirit of God and not in the flesh, which can easily deceive us.

Integrity protects a person (Proverbs 10:9). Saul lacked integrity and lost his kingdom. Daniel, however, stood firm in integrity and was exalted (Daniel 6:4). In modern times, scandals in politics and business show the high cost of dishonesty. Integrity in leaders and individuals builds trust, stability, and blessings.

CHAPTER 14:

THE DISOBEDIENCE OF STEWARDSHIP

God entrusts resources, talents, and time to every person. Disobedience of stewardship is wasting, misusing, or neglecting these gifts. "As every man hath received the gift, even so minister the same one to another, as good stewards of the manifold grace of God (1 Peter 4:10)." Stewardship is an honor that relays the message of God's trust in humanity. Adam was given the stewardship of the Garden of Eden, and ever since, we have been blessed to steward God's creation and our own responsibilities. Have we failed in our stewardship towards God and man? Has the manifold grace of God been revoked because of sin and disobedience? Certainly not!

Today, in an era shaped by polarized ideologies, bureaucratic inertia, and algorithmic conformity, disobedience is not simply an act of resistance—it is a form of thinking. It reflects moral clarity, emotional courage, and cognitive integrity. Neuroscience and philosophy are converging on the same insight: disobedience is not a failure of discipline, but a sign of preserved humanity (Clara H. Whyte). This perspective is not good, and stewardship of our thinking and behavior must not be initiated by disobedience. Disobedience has no positive results or outcome. The only cognitive response is rebellion and refusal to obey a rule, commandment or decree.

The parable of the talents in Matthew 25 illustrates this. There were three servants given five talents, two talents and one talent. The servant who received the five talents went and produced five more; a good steward was he. And likewise, the servant with two talents when and gained two more, another good steward. Unfortunately, the servant with the one talent buried his talent in fear, was condemned, while those who invested wisely were rewarded. A great lesson is expounded on the talents, resources, skills, and abilities we have been given and blessed with by God. In utilizing, functioning and producing greater as Jesus stated, we become good and faithful servants of the Lord. When we are disobedient to our stewardship, we become wicked and slothful servants of ourselves.

Jesus conveyed another parable in Luke 16 regarding the unjust steward. The steward was accused of wasting his Master's goods and had to give an account of his stewardship. What would you do if you had to give an account to God at this very moment? So, the steward became methodical and called all his Master's debtors, reducing their debts so he might gain their favor. Although his Master commended him in his wise craftiness, he was still unrighteous in his actions. "He that is faithful in that which is least is faithful also in much: and he that is unjust in the least is unjust also in much. If therefore ye have not been faithful in the unrighteous mammon, who will commit to your trust the true riches (Luke 16:10-11)?" We must never be unjust, even if we lose everything. Thus, it has resulted in the unjust of today. Many are stealing, taking advantage of the weak, and leaving others without resources.

In Luke 12:16-21, Jesus speaks another parable of the rich fool. In the time of wealth, millionaires, and billionaires, and of poor people, this parable exhibits the world's greed and focuses not on God or on their stewardship. The rich man said to himself that he had so much money that he did not know what to do with it. Instead of seeking the needs of others and the kingdom of God, he decided to build more barns to store his wealth. Building more houses in America has become a problem for the stewardship of trees, the environment, and ecosystems. This disobedience has caused all kinds of health issues, shortenings of life, and pollution. "But God said unto him, Thou fool, this night thy soul shall be required of thee: then whose shall those things be, which thou hast provided? So is he that layeth up treasure for himself, and is not rich toward God (Luke 12:20-21)." Riches come, and they fly away like the wind. We will all have to give an account to God one day, and greed may not be good stewardship.

Disobedience in stewardship leads to loss, lack, and judgment. Obedience in stewardship brings increase, blessing, and honor. "Every act of stewardship on earth has an eternal dimension to it as well. While we may see immediate outcomes here, there's a lasting impact that transcends our earthly existence (Rick). Many people have lost positions, family trust, and possessions due to disobedience to stewardship, and the consequences have been devastating to the unjust steward's mental, physical, spiritual, and emotional well-being. Furthermore, a lack of respect, trust, interactions, and investing in the character of the unfaithful steward is another reason society failed to come together on one accord. The one thing individuals tend to overlook is that just because the result of the consequence did not happen immediately, it will still come.

We are called to steward our finances, relationships, time, and environment faithfully. "And the Lord said, Who then is that faithful and wise steward, whom his lord shall make ruler over his household, to give them their portion of meat in due season? Blessed is that servant, whom his lord when he cometh shall find so doing (Luke 12:42-43)." In good stewardship, we are also commanded to teach and share wisdom about finances, relationships, and any other knowledge that helps develop good stewardship. Stewardship is not just about being a good servant; it is at the heart of bearing good fruit and striving to do our best for God and the well-being of one another. In addition, our individual contribution keeps disobedience from destroying plants, animals, marine life, and humanity. It is in our response to God's calling that we are obeying and carrying forth His purpose.

Jesus taught the parable of the talents (Matthew 25:14–30). The servant who buried his gift was judged, while faithful servants were rewarded. Today, the misuse of money, time, or resources shows a lack of stewardship. Faithful stewardship, however, brings increase, prosperity, and eternal reward.

CHAPTER 15:

THE PATH BACK TO OBEDIENCE

Though disobedience brings consequences, there is always a path back to the loving arms of God the Father through Jesus Christ the Son. Repentance is the first step—turning away from sin and returning to God. 1 John 1:9 promises, "If we confess our sins, he is faithful and just to forgive us and purify us from all unrighteousness." Turning away is more than saying "I will not do it anymore." A renewing of the mind and a heart set to seek God is where true repentance takes possession. After confession and repentance have taken root, justification and sanctification can transform the sinner into a saint, the unrighteous into the righteous, and the disobedient into the obedient.

The second step is surrender—yielding to God's will in humility and trust. In our own will, the call to yield is impossible, but through the asking of the Holy Spirit, daily help comes when we surrender; furthermore, in dying daily to self and crucifying the flesh, power is surrendered to Jesus. The third step is obedience—walking daily in alignment with His Word and Spirit. There is a hymn that says, "trust and obey, there is no other way." "Can two walk together, except they be agreed (Amos 3:3)? We have to agree with every word God has spoken and walk in the Spirit that manifests the truth. Only in obedience will we walk in alignment, in spirit and in truth.

God has said through the Apostle Peter, "the Lord is not slack concerning his promise, as some men count slackness; but is longsuffering to us-ward, not willing that any should perish, but that all should come to repentance (2 Peter 3:9)." God has been very patience and gracious to us and He wants a relationship with all those who are obedient. Jesus is waiting for us to come to Him so that He can put us back on the path to obedience and abundant life. Furthermore, "because strait is the gate, and narrow is the way, which leadeth unto life, and few there be that find it (Matthew 7:14)." The path is narrow, but thanks be to God that we don't have to travel alone or be misled by anything or anyone that would deter us from being obedient and pressing forward toward the high calling of God (Philippians 3:14).

The story of the Prodigal Son beautifully illustrates this path. Though he disobeyed and squandered his inheritance, he returned to his father in repentance and was restored with love and honor. Likewise, we, in our own selfish hearts, make choices just as the Prodigal Son did, and, like him, we soon discover what life is really like without God. The word prodigal ("ἄσωτος") means to be wasteful, and we know that is disobedience to stewardship and other principles. Nevertheless, the story of the Prodigal Son is gleaming with lessons and truths about God's forgiveness, love and restoration. In verse 20, we read that the father saw his son afar off, ran, fell on his neck, and kissed him. That's God's heart towards a child ready to surrender, repent, obey and be restored in the kingdom of God.

No matter how far disobedience has taken us, God's grace is greater. The cross of Christ is the ultimate expression of God's willingness to forgive and restore. Through Christ, we can walk in obedience, experience blessing, and live with purpose. He is waiting with open arms to receive all who are willing to come and take up their cross and follow Him in obedience. Moreover, Christ is our only hope for eternal life.

The journey of obedience is not about perfection but about direction. On the journey, if you're following directions and being obedient, perfection is about making you complete and bringing glory to God. Each day is an opportunity to choose obedience, to walk in faith, and to honor God with our lives. The journey will have its challenges, trials and tribulations; however, an obedient lifestyle will always give you the confidence and strength to overcome and find joy. The journey can take us off the path of Adam and Eve in disobedience and put us on the path of Noah, who found favor in God's eyes, and of Abraham, who was called a friend of God because his faith was counted as righteousness. Both were obedient to God's voice.

Repentance restores fellowship with God (1 John 1:9). The Prodigal Son returned and was welcomed (Luke 15:11-24). Steps to obedience include confession, surrender, faith, and daily obedience.

Modern testimonies of addicts, leaders, and families restored through repentance show that no one is too far gone. Through Christ, obedience is possible, and His grace is greater than all disobedience.

CONCLUSION

Disobedience is costly. It separates us from God, harms relationships, weakens societies, and brings destruction. Yet, obedience brings blessing, life, and restoration. This book has explored the many dimensions of disobedience and its consequences, but it has also shown the hope of redemption.

The path of obedience is not always easy, but it is always worth it. To walk in obedience is to walk in alignment with the God who loves us, protects us, and desires our good. May we choose obedience, not disobedience, and experience the fullness of life that God has promised.

REFERENCES

All Scripture is taken from the King James Version otherwise notated.

Bible Hub, 2004-2025. Saul's Disobedience. https://biblehub.com/topical/s/saul's_disobedience.htm

Jill Baker, Brian Houseman, Alice Matthews. 2014. David's Disobedience to God Causes a National Pestilence (1 Chronicles 21:1-17). https://www.theologyofwork.org/old-testament/samuel-kings-chronicles-and-work/the-golden-age-of-the-monarchy-2-samuel-1-24-1-kings-1-11-1-chronicles-21-2/davids-successes-and-failures-as-king-2-samuel-1-24/davids-disobedience-to-god-causes-a-national-pestilence-1-chronicles-211-17

Walter A. Elwell. 1996. Baker's Evangelical Dictionary of Biblical Theology. https://www.biblestudytools.com/dictionary/law/. Baker Book House Company, Grand Rapids, Michigan USA.

Fr. Ed Broom, OMV. 2025. To Become Holy as the Father is Holy. https://catholicexchange.com/to-become-holy-as-the-father-is-holy/

Bible Hub. https://www.biblehub.com/1_corinthians/15-33.htm

CrossTalk. 2025. What are the consequences of lacking faith in God? https://crosstalk.ai/knowledgebase/wellbeing/spiritual-wellbeing/what-consequences-lacking-faith-god/

Steven J. Cole. 2018. 24. The Tragic Consequences of Unbelief (Numbers 14:11-45). https://bible.org/seriespage/24-tragic-consequences-unbelief-numbers-1411-45Morris I. Leibman. 1992. Civil Disobedience: A Threat to Our Society Under Law. https://fee.org/articles/civil-disobedience-a-threat-to-our-society-under-law/

NTF. 2023. How does corruption affects society and what are its effects? https://www.thentf.org/article/how-does-corruption-affects-society-and-what-are-its-effects/

Focus on the Family. Truth Rising | Full Documentary. https://www.youtube.com/watch?v=XXc5IhgSZkg

Rev. Samuel Arimoro. 2025. CONSEQUENCES OF DISOBEDIENCE IN LEADERSHIP. https://samuelarimoro.wordpress.com/2025/07/05/consequences-of-disobedience-in-leadership/

Doug Thorpe. 2023. Should a Leader Challenge or Disobey Orders from Higher Authorities? https://dougthorpe.com/should-a-leader-challenge-or-disobey-orders-from-higher-authorities/

Colin Tan. 2023. 20 Fatherless Homes Statistics in 2025 (U.S. & World). https://increditools.com/fatherless-homes-statistics/

Pastor David. 2025. 2 Chronicles 15:6 Meaning & Explanation (with Related Verses). https://christianitypath.com/2-chronicles-15-6/

Nathan Millican. 2017. Unbelief abuses truth through a deliberate act of suppression. https://theologyalongtheway.org/2017/07/31/unbelief-abuses-truth-through-a-deliberate-act-of-suppression/

Bing.com. 2025. https://www.bing.com/search?q=disobedience+of+truth&qs=

NW_QB&pq=disobedience+of+tru&sk=CGS2NM1&sc=11-19&cvid=D3739749757B4C7C9FD356E493D34D2B&FORM=QBRE&sp=4&ghc=1&lq=0&ntref=1

Clara H. Whyte, M.A. 2025. The Science of Courage: Why Disobedience Is Vital for Human Dignity and Freedom. https://www.linkedin.com/pulse/science-courage-why-disobedience-vital-human-dignity-clara-h--1plee/

Rick Pina. 2023. The Positive & Negative Consequences of Stewardship. http://todaysword.org/2023/09/22/the-positive-negative-consequences-of-stewardship/

www.ingramcontent.com/pod-product-compliance
Lightning Source LLC
Chambersburg PA
CBHW051900090426
42811CB00003B/410